Important Notice!

No animals were harmed in the making of this book.

OK, we did test a couple of chapters on Libby the Cat, but we're fairly sure that she did not sustain any long-term psychological damage.

Of course, she was pretty messed up to start with.

To Kathleen
a fellow word-wrangler
Enjoy!

WHAT I'VE LEARNED SO FAR...

Part I:

Bikes, Docks & Slush Nuggets

Mike Ball

What I've Learned So Far...
Part I: Bikes, Docks & Slush Nuggets

Copyright © 2009 by Michael Ball
All rights reserved.
No part of this book may be reproduced or transmitted in any form or by any means, electronic or mechanical, including photocopying, recording, or by any information storage and retrieval system, without written permission from the author.

Cover Illustration by Riccardo Capraro

Cover Design by Thomas Pulling

Visit our Web site at http://learnedsofar.com for more information.

ISBN: 1-4392-6209-8

Library of Congress Control Number:
2009911189

*To my Dad, who never quite managed
get his arms around his dreams.*

Acknowledgements

I owe this book, and all the years of the weekly What I've Learned So Far... columns to:

- My family, especially my wife Nancy and son Patrick, who not only have to live with me, they have had to put up with me telling the world about nearly everything they do.

- Scott Lorenz, my publicist, strategic brain trust, and the best friend I could ever hope to have.

- My dear mate Tom Pulling, who not only helped with the visual design for the book, he is the infamous "Tom" of various adventures you'll find scattered throughout these pages.

- My old friend Riccardo Capraro, who did the cover illustration for this book, and who just might be the most talented artist on the planet.

- My Editor and friend, Yvonne Lorenz, who has infinite patience with me and who somehow knows that "principle" is different than "principal." Huh!

- And to all my readers, who have constantly been willing to write in and remind me that I am well and truly a world-class Dork.

Introduction

OK, so here's the deal. I'm just like you - if you happen to be a middle-aged guy living in the Midwestern United States with an infinitely tolerant wife, some more-or-less domesticated animals, and pretty much no clue.

I've raised a son and shared my personal values with him, coached his hockey teams, taught him to belch at will, and made sure that the analyst he will go to someday will enjoy decades of steady income. Among other things, I have discovered that you can actually see the cloud of testosterone hovering overhead in a high school hockey team's locker room.

Over the years I played a little ice hockey myself, which went a long way toward filling up my Frequent Customer card at the physical therapist. I'm a pretty good scuba diver, a really bad golfer, and the worst bowler who ever tried to look nonchalant after dropping a sixteen pound bowling ball on his foot.

A few years ago I won some trophies as a pairs water skier. This sport is a lot like pairs figure skating, only with less Russian mafia involvement. During my career I had four lovely and unbelievably patient partners, Amanda, Megan, Sarah and Brittany, all of whom thought it was pretty funny that they could con me into going out in public wearing brightly colored spandex. My job was to do the skiing and to keep the girls looking pretty up over my head.

I started playing the guitar when I was a kid, with the express goal of becoming Rick Nelson. Since then I've made varying amounts of money playing guitars, banjos, ukuleles, trumpets, harmonicas, jaw harps, drums, and plastic shaker eggs. Just for the record, that Rick Nelson thing never really worked out.

One amazing thing that came out of my life as a musician has been the opportunity to work with incarcerated and at-risk kids through a group called Lost Voices. Along with outstanding touring musicians like Kitty Donohoe, Josh White, Jr. and Peter Madcat Ruth, I go into facilities for troubled young people, where we help them explore their lives by writing and performing folk and blues music. You can learn more about Lost Voices at www.lostvoices.org.

For most of my adult life I have earned my living putting words on paper. Some of it was advertising copy - headlines, jingles, speeches, white papers, pamphlets, Web sites, and even a eulogy for a dog. I was the creator of hard-hitting, nail-biting marketing prose like:

Turbo Upgrades can give your 8mm tape drive the capacity it needs to keep up with the rest of your mass storage system!

Now I'm just guessing here, but I feel like 300 pages of that kind of stuff might not have made for much of a book.

As luck would have it, I also took a little time along the way to jot down a few notes about things that were going on around me, then publish them in newspapers, magazines, and online all over the world. For the past seven years these columns have appeared under the title, *What I've Learned So Far...*

In 2003 I had the great honor of receiving the Erma Bombeck Award.

Please note that this book has been thoroughly Throne Tested - every entry is optimized, in length and content, to be read on the crapper. Oh, and if you really can't stand the suspense, you can learn what "Slush Nuggets" are on Page 17.

And now, read on and check out some of the things that I've managed to learn - so far.

Part I: Bikes, Docks & Slush Nuggets

Just A Little Bike

*This is the column that won the
2002 Erma Bombeck Award.*

The other day I dropped off my son's little bike at the church rummage sale.

This is the little bike with special knurled steel pegs sticking out of the front axle, pegs my son could stand on so he could, for reasons obvious only to him, bounce and pirouette the bike on its front wheel.

This is the little bike that had no kickstand, and no fenders, and no trim of any kind, because these things would add weight, and weight is to be avoided at all costs when the whole idea of a little bike is to defy the laws of physics.

This is the little bike with a knobby back tire so my son could get good traction on the dirt path in the woods leading up to the ramp made of mud, gravel, and a school cafeteria tray, a ramp which would launch him in a soaring arc across the four foot wide Creek of Doom.

This is the bike with the really neat graphic of a raptor on the frame; I can still see its reflection in my son's eyes the first time he saw the bike. Now there are bits of raptor missing, matching up with various "road rash" scars on my son's body, places where some paint and some skin were lost each time the bike and the boy just missed clearing that creek.

This is the little bike that was my son's steed every day, until the day he got his driver's license. On that day he left behind that world where you fly over creeks, and you duck under branches, and you pedal until your skin gets so hot it glows.

This is the little bike that sat in the shed under the deck for four years, transformed overnight from the center of my son's universe into a mobile hanger for the extension cord. It's chain got rusty. It's tires went flat. The raptor gradually disappeared under a coat of dust.

This is the little bike I dragged out of the shed, and wiped off the dust, and pumped up the tires, and oiled the chain, and took to the church. There was nobody around to hear me say good-bye to it or to see the tears in my eyes when I dropped it off.

Part I: Bikes, Docks & Slush Nuggets

Today at the rummage sale I saw a young father listening patiently as his ten-year-old son explained the knurled pegs on the front axle, and the knobby back tire, and the really neat graphic of a raptor on the frame, and why there was no kickstand, and all the other reasons my son's little bike should go home with them.

And now it's his son's little bike.

A Perfect Christmas Day

6:15 AM – The bedroom door swings open and Todd Junior launches himself onto the bed screaming, "Mom! Dad! Wake Up! IT'S CHRISTMAS!"

Dad, who was assembling and wrapping toys until twenty minutes ago, can't open his eyes, so he groans something fortunately unintelligible.

"I told him not to come in here," shrieks Little Suzie from the doorway, nearly hitting that elusive B-above-high-C, and sending Bernie the Schnauzer into convulsions. "I told him he had to wait until the sun came up!"

"It's Christmas, it's Christmas, it's Ca-Ca-Ca-Ca-Christmas," chants Todd Junior, marching in pajama-footed cadence back and forth across Dad's chest.

"I'll make some coffee" says Mom, pulling on her robe.

6:45 AM – The living room has been transformed from a holiday fairyland into a red-and-green battlefield, strewn with torn paper, empty boxes and discarded stick-on bows. Dad now has one eye open and is trying to reattach the head of Little Suzie's brand new "Burping Bernice" doll, accidentally decapitated during the debut of Todd Junior's life-size "Johnny Bayonet Charge" play set. Bernie the Schnauzer has chewed up and swallowed his new "Lasts For Years" Teflon bone.

7:15 AM – Little Suzie is busy configuring the tiny computer network in her new "Barbie's Penthouse Office Suite," while Todd Junior has just discovered that his new toy fire truck is fairly ineffective in combating the experimental tissue-paper blaze he touched off with Mom's new aromatherapy candle.

Mom is making more coffee.

12:00 Noon – With both children asleep under the tree in nests of shattered toys, Dad unconscious in his chair, and Mom putting the finishing touches on her famous three-bean casserole, the family starts to arrive. Great Aunt Ellen and Great Uncle Charlie show up bearing a cake, a three-bean casserole, Carl The Dog, and a

What I've Learned So Far...

garbage bag full of gifts.

12:15 PM – Aunt Karen, Uncle Fred, Sheldon, and Brittany help Grandma and Grandpa bring in a pumpkin pie, an apple pie, two three-bean casseroles, and a garbage bag full of gifts.

12:20 PM – Uncle Stan and his girlfriend Stacey arrive with a plate of cookies, a three-bean casserole, and two garbage bags full of gifts.

12:28 PM – Aunt Meg, Uncle Bob, Pammie, and the Twins come to the door with a mincemeat pie, a three-bean casserole, and a garbage bag full of garbage.

12:29 PM – Uncle Bob heads back home to get the garbage bag full of gifts from his driveway next to the dumpster, while the women sip coffee in the kitchen and try to sort out just who was supposed to bring three-bean casserole and who was supposed to bring the ham.

1:05 PM – Dad, Uncle Bob and Uncle Fred set out to try to find a store open on Christmas day that might sell hams. Todd Junior, Sheldon and the Twins are in the backyard planning to "Johnny Bayonet Charge" the girls, not yet realizing that Little Suzie has deadbolted them out of the house. The girls are in the living room playing "Investment Banker Barbie."

Mom makes more coffee.

3:18 PM – The men come home with eighteen small tins of canned corned beef and a bag of Twizzlers they picked up at a truck stop on the interstate. Grandpa, dressed head-to-foot in flannel, wool, and thermal long johns, has found the thermostat in the living room, and the fish tank is starting to simmer.

3:22 PM – The boys have finally made it back into the house and Aunt Meg is checking them for signs of frostbite. The girls are locked in Little Suzie's room planning Barbie's campaign for the state legislature. The dogs are in the dining room eating the ham that they found in the bottom of Grandma and Grandpa's bag of gifts.

Mom makes more coffee.

4:00 PM – The Family sits down to a Christmas feast of canned corned beef and three-bean casserole. Mom bites right through her coffee mug, so she switches to White Zinfandel.

4:45 PM – More presents! Great Aunt Ellen bought each of the children an identical orange stocking cap, with ribs knitted into them so that they stick straight up. Apparently mistaking the kids for seven wool-topped traffic cones, the dogs slalom joyfully through them, while the adults open their gifts with unbridled enthusiasm;

"Wow! A Dandruff Sentry! How did you know?"

11:30 PM – The football games (at least the important ones) are over. The gifts are redistributed into their garbage bags to go home, and the kids are draped lifelessly over parents' shoulders. Ten gallons of three-bean casserole are congealing in the garbage can.

And all is right with the world.

Part I: Bikes, Docks & Slush Nuggets

Guidelines For Snowbirds

Two kinds of people live in Michigan in the winter. There are those who manage to go South and get warm for a while, who we'll call "Snowbirds," and there are those who don't, who we'll call "Clinically Depressed."

I don't count people who go to Hawaii, which is clearly not "South." These people are in a third category, and we'll call them "Arrogant Pampered Jerks." I'd really rather not talk about them.

Now if you've lived around here for any length of time, you've probably found yourself in one category or the other depending on the year – some winters you get a little time in the sun, and some winters you don't. When I don't, I try not to begrudge all those luckier folks, because I figure sooner or later my turn might come around again, and I don't want to be getting all begrudged.

What I've Learned So Far...

So I was as gracious as I could manage last week when my friend called me from Florida, just as I got home from work. "Hey man," I said, cheerfully stomping the ice out of the treads of my sneakers, "How's the Sunny South?"

"It rained for over an hour today. Can you believe it?"

"Oh, I'm sorry to hear that," I replied, sympathetically shaking the snow out of my jacket and hair. "Well, at least it's warm down there."

"Warm! It barely got to seventy-five degrees today!"

"That's too bad," I said, chipping the ice out of my wrist watch and rubbing my hands together to see if I could get any feeling back in them. "That must have been really hard on you guys. Seventy-five – brrrrr!"

"And the temperature really dropped when the sun went down. I may have to wear a windbreaker to dinner tonight!"

"Wow, Dude, that really sucks," I said, sitting next to the puddle of slush by the back door and picking the little ice balls off my socks. "Good idea to wear a windbreaker, though. You don't want to catch a chill."

After I got off the phone, I decided that it might be useful to jot down a few things that you Snowbirds might think about when you feel the

Part I: Bikes, Docks & Slush Nuggets

need to communicate with the rest of us:

1. On the way home tonight I watched a panel truck slide off an icy overpass and take out a busload of nuns. Don't call and complain to me that the little umbrella fell into your Mai Tai.

2. If the Victoria's Secret models are staying at your hotel and rehearsing for an all-thong fashion show out by the pool, don't tell me about it. Just get pictures and as much video footage as you can, so we can discuss it when you get home.

3. Bear in mind that I'm comforting myself with the idea that I'm saving the big bucks you're spending on your vacation. Please don't tell me that your boss gave you the keys to his fully-stocked condo, round-trip air fare, and a lotto ticket that hit for ten thousand bucks that you're using for walking-around money.

4. My back is sore from shoveling 2,400 pounds of snow out of the driveway so I could go out and get my car stuck in the bank parking lot. I'm not interested in hearing that your back is sore from playing that extra eighteen holes of golf. The same goes for your aches and pains from tennis, water skiing, scuba diving, or surfing. Unless you got bit by an alligator or a shark – that might make me feel a little bit better.

Just remember – in another week or two, you'll be back in Michigan, slogging around in the frozen muck like the rest of us. And I think you'll find that the new sun tan you're sporting is pretty much irrelevant when you're out there hacking the ice off your windshield at 6:30 in the morning. That's right, Sun Seeker, you gotta come home sometime.

    Until then, try to be kind.

Part I: Bikes, Docks & Slush Nuggets

The Snowbirds Revenge

Last week my column was about Snowbirds, those uncaring people who send us cute postcards from Florida while we're up here chipping the snot icicles off our upper lips. It seems that there are a few people who didn't completely agree with the tone of my piece. Some sounded just a little bit angry:

Dear Mr. Funny Guy,

You got a lot of nerve! Why I ought to rip your head off and crap down your neck, you no good commie...

Well, you get the idea.

My favorite letter came from Mrs. Alma Thigwump, who lives in the area with her husband Floyd and their three boys. Mrs. Thigwump said that we non-snowbirds should really try not to be envious.

What I've Learned So Far...

To reinforce this, she sent me a copy of her personal journal of the family's winter vacation to Ft. Lauderdale. Here are a few excerpts:

Day 1 – *Gosh, the airport security isn't nearly as terrible as everybody's been saying. Billy threw up on the lady who was running the x-ray machine, but the lines weren't nearly as bad as I expected.*

The flight was great, until Floyd Junior locked himself in the bathroom and tried to flush his backpack down that little steel toilet. The flight attendant told me that the blue stuff will probably stain his clothes, but that it should wash right out of his hair.

The claims agent assured us that the airline didn't lose our bags. They sent them to Guam.

Day 2 – *We all got lots of sun today – good thing I packed the SPF 30! Our hotel is beautiful, with palm trees and flowers all around the pool. Tommy threw up in the pool.*

There seems to be some sort of cat living in our room, but we can't seem to catch it or even get a good look at it.

Day 3 – *It rained today. The cat in our room turned out to be a nine pound cockroach – Floyd hit it with his shoe, and it hit him back. We all waited down in the lobby while the manager took his rifle up and shot it.*

Also, it seems that Floyd Junior had replaced the SPF 30 sun screen with Wesson Oil. The doctor says that the blisters will probably go down in a couple of days, then we'll all start peeling.

Billy threw up on the doctor.

Day 4 – *It's still raining. We went to the mall to buy some underwear, since ours are in Guam. Tommy and Billy took turns throwing up in Starbucks, and Floyd Junior went swimming in the fountain. The doctor says the rash should go away in a week or so.*

Day 5 – *We went out to breakfast at the cutest little diner just down the road from the hotel. Floyd Junior threw up on an elderly couple while we were waiting for a table.*

We all had pancakes.

The sun came out for a couple of hours this afternoon, so we all went to play miniature golf. They hope to have Billy extracted from the windmill by supper time.

Day 6 – *Nobody threw up today!*

Since the weather has been bad, the kids have used the Pay-Per-View in the room quite a bit. So far we've paid $696.15 to watch Freddy vs. Jason one hundred and seventeen times.

Day 7 – *Well, our vacation is over. Our suitcases were delivered to the hotel this morning, just in time for us to go to the airport and check them through back to Guam.*

We sure will miss Florida, but we're all glad to be heading home, where the kids can vomit in their own beds.

Ok, Mrs. Thigwump. You win. I stand corrected.

Part I: Bikes, Docks & Slush Nuggets

Treasures of Spring

Each Spring, as Old Man Winter starts thinking about getting his frosty white butt out of town for Spring Break, we Michiganonians (Michigaroonies? I hate being called a "Michigander") begin to experience a phenomenon that's unique to states where we spend four months out of every year walking around in stupid-looking little wool hats and wearing our socks to bed.

I'm talking about Slush Nuggets.

In case you've never heard of them, "Slush Nuggets" are those great little treasures that show up in your yard as the snow melts. I live on a busy street, where the snowplows push their grimy little glaciers up into my yard all winter long. By the time March rolls around I've accumulated a pretty substantial heap of road slop, and a particularly rich haul of Slush Nuggets.

Now I'm not really talking about the Almond Joy wrappers and peppermint schnapps bottles that always seem to poke their way out of the drifts after every gala Saturday night. These would fall more into the category of "Trash." And, of course there are the occasional zoological discoveries, which I probably should technically refer to as "Roadkill."

No, I'm talking about the riches that transform the chore of cleaning up the lawn every Spring into a mini-adventure in social anthropology.

Bear in mind that when I say "riches," it's the cultural, not the monetary value of Slush Nuggets that is significant. Oh sure, there was the rear-view mirror from that 1997 Hyundai that turned out to be worth more than the replacement value of the entire car, but that's a pretty rare find. Normally, what makes a Slush Nugget special is the implied story. Each artifact represents a tiny vignette of someone's life.

For instance, there was the paper plate with the name "Candy" and a phone number written on it in lipstick. Instantly, the name "Candy" conjures images of big hair, lots of eye makeup, and possibly a couple of surgically-enhanced body

Part I: Bikes, Docks & Slush Nuggets

parts. Gazing at this artifact, you can actually visualize a young couple coming together across a smoky pool table - their eyes meet; she scrawls her phone number on the paper plate the very second someone polishes off the last mozzarella stick; he takes it from her greasy hand and presses it to his heart.

The phone number turned out to be (honest Honey, I just called it as research for the column) the number of a pizza delivery store. Maybe, I thought, Candy just wanted to make sure that her new friend had a handy way to deal with any sort of "hunger" situation he might encounter.

The fact that the plate ended up in my yard tells me that ordering a pizza wasn't really what he had in mind.

Of course some of the stories behind my Slush Nuggets are a bit more puzzling. For instance how, when the wind chill is fifteen degrees below zero, would someone not notice losing a shoe? Or a pair of boxer shorts? Or their bra? You would think that cold toes would be a dead giveaway. Or the draft.

The Slush Nuggets I'm currently trying to interpret include a box of crayons with all the tips bitten off, an unopened jar of anchovies, a toupee (very nearly mis-categorized as "Roadkill" since it was pretty much the same color and texture as a squashed muskrat), an eyeglass case containing a pair of cardboard 3-D glasses, and an inexpensive picture frame with a photograph of someone's belly button mounted in it (the belly button was an "innie").

Who says winters in Michigan are not entertaining?

Part I: Bikes, Docks & Slush Nuggets

No More Mr. Fixit

Some guys are "handy," in the sense that if you give one of them a hammer he will be able to hold it in his "hand" without dropping it through a glass coffee table. If you ask him to fix a leak under the sink he can fix it without having to replace the entire west half of the house. If you need a loose screw tightened he can do it without necessarily drawing blood.

I am not one of those handy guys. I believe that if God had intended for me to use a screwdriver, he would have given me the ability. Or at least the desire.

A handy guy is easy to spot in his natural habitat. Within an hour of moving into a house that most people would consider perfectly satisfactory, he will have the bathtub sitting out in the driveway, filled with all the old wiring and light fixtures from the family room. He just can't leave well enough alone.

On the other hand, I firmly believe that "alone" is absolutely where you should leave well enough. This philosophy makes life a lot simpler for me and millions of other fixit-challenged men. For instance, if there is a blemish on a wall – like a hole from, say, a nail or a mortar round – the handy guy will rebuild the wall, maybe adding on a spare bathroom while he's at it. I'll just hang a picture over the hole – or maybe a poster in the case of the mortar round.

The irony here is that, like all men, I have the "Cool Tool Gene," meaning that I love wandering around in Sears, saying things like, "Wow! That four and a half horse Briggs and Stratton sure will give this baby a real kick in the butt!"

I can spend hours gazing at drills, log splitters, table saws, and air compressors. I think tools, especially the ones that represent substantial destructive capacity, are terrific, and I even own some. I just know better than to ever try to turn them on without proper supervision.

Now it may seem ideal to live with a handy guy. After all, if the dog digs a hole in the back yard, this man will dig it out a little more and turn it into a swimming pool.

Part I: Bikes, Docks & Slush Nuggets

The only drawback is that handy guys never seem to get anything completely finished. Two years after the dog kicks off that project, there might be water in the pool, but Mr. Buildit is still trying to round up enough plutonium for the nuclear pool heater.

Please notice that I'm just talking about men, on both ends of the handiness spectrum. This is because women who are handy are usually not obsessive about it. If a light switch needs to be fixed and a woman knows how to do it, she will quietly take care of it without bringing down the Midwest power grid. And if she doesn't know how to do it, she will quietly call an electrician.

So I have a message for all you handy guys out there. Just because you know how to "sweat a joint" in a water pipe – or even know what that means – doesn't mean that you have to go around doing it.

No Green Thumb Either

Ok, so the ice is off the lake and only two of my dock poles and my neighbor's paddle boat went out with it. It's Spring! Time for me to dig right in and avoid working in the yard!

If you are acquainted with me at all, you will know that I am pretty much pathologically tool-challenged. This disability extends to gardening tools, power or otherwise, so if you happen to see me out "puttering" in the yard, you would be well advised to take cover. I've actually broken a window with the head flying off my leaf rake.

What brings this to mind is that I saw one of my neighbors outside today, "de-thatching" his yard. He had a little gas-powered machine that was apparently designed to dig out all the old dead grass and leave it there like mown hay, so

Part I: Bikes, Docks & Slush Nuggets

he could come back around later and rake it up. "I already took ten bags out of the back yard," he said proudly.

"Wow, way to go," I replied. "And what in the name of Weed 'N Feed would possess you to do that?"

"It aerates the lawn," he explained. "Otherwise, you're going to have all that thatch down there choking your roots."

"Well we sure as heck don't want that, do we?" I said, trying to fully absorb the thought of all my roots down there, gasping for breath.

I toyed briefly with the idea of running right home and de-thatching my own lawn. After all, my neighbor's little machine did look pretty cool, and it made a whole bunch of noise. Fortunately for everyone concerned, I almost immediately came to my senses.

We have a simple system at our house – if it's alive, my wife is in charge. How this rule applies to the animals (and it does!) will be the subject of future discussion, but suffice it to say that all the plants, from the grass to the geraniums, fall under her benevolent protection.

I am allowed to cut the grass, since the plants my wife doesn't want summarily cut down are protected by stout mower-proof landscape timbers, and because you can do relatively little damage with a lawn mower (you can do almost unbelievable damage to a lawn mower, but that's another subject for future discussion).

I'm also permitted to do a limited amount of hedge trimming, fertilizing and spreading of weed killers, all under strict supervision.

The rationale for our system is obvious. I have trouble telling a daffodil from a dandelion, so I'm really not the ideal candidate for weeding the flower garden. I can kill any plant just by spending a little time alone in a room with it. When the moles moved in and turned our lawn into an underground Grand Prix race course, I wanted to name the cute little guys and teach them some tricks.

I once lost control of a roto-tiller and left the yard looking like the aftermath of a carpet bombing.

Now all you women are saying, "He only pretends to be helpless so he can get out of doing all the yard work." To that I say, "Geeze, what a great idea! Why, that could work for laundry, or washing dishes, or cleaning, or almost anything!

Thanks for the tip, ladies!"

Beer And Engineering

The Egyptians engineered the Pyramids. The Romans engineered the Coliseum. Somebody or other apparently engineered Stonehenge. And a couple of weeks ago, my friend Tom and I engineered The Dock.

For us The Dock represents a sacred ritual of spring – kind of like sacrificing a goat, only with a little less bloodshed, and you don't get any lamb chops when you're done.

It's a ritual we like to perform just as early in the season as we possibly can. Now any rational individual – and by "rational individual" I mean "my wife" – might question the logic in putting on a pair of waders and spending hours splashing around in 40 degree water, when we could simply wait a few weeks until the water gets warm.

Huh!

What I've Learned So Far...

So anyway, on the first halfway decent Saturday every spring Tom and I assemble all the essential dock-installing equipment – a couple of wrenches and a six pack – and go to work.

The first step is to lay out a careful plan. This consists mostly of gesturing with the neck of a beer bottle toward a pile of unidentifiable (by us) metal parts and saying, "I don't remember those. Was all that stuff here last year?"

Next comes the installation of the ceremonial First Section. This always takes a while, because it requires carefully leveling the bank and building a foundation of rocks and beer cans.

Then we firmly set the first set of poles. After this stage is complete, we often get as many as three or four additional sections put in before the whole deal collapses.

Gazing at the wreckage, we develop a theory that if we just had ourselves a different kind of bracket thingy and a better brand of beer, the whole job would be much more efficient. A trip to the store and several hours of changing bracket thingies later, we're back in the water gazing at more wreckage.

Following much discussion and pointing with the necks of bottles, we discover that the new bracket thingies are the exact same kind we threw away last year because they kept making the whole deal collapse.

And so it goes. Finally, after many more hours and trips to the store, we have what might potentially be a sound dock structure. The only remaining step is to send one of the kids walking out there to test it.

Now you may wonder why this Beer and Engineering process remains so complicated year after year. If you don't, our wives sure do. "It seems like you two idiots would eventually get a clue," is how they express it. Our response is very simple – don't hold your breath.

And so, in the gathering dusk the following conversation marks the end of every successful dock building project:

"Man, what a great dock," I say.

"It sure is," says Tom.

(The sound of bottles clinking together in a victory toast.)

"Let's label all the parts so we know just how to do it next year."

"Great idea! And we'll take pictures of everything, so we'll have a record of exactly how it all goes together."

"Right. But we can do that later. After all, we have all summer."

(Bottles clinking together in another toast.)

Thrills and Grills

I'm an excellent cook.

Ok, I'll admit it – saying that is a lot like Dustin Hoffman's character in Rain Man saying, "I'm an excellent driver." To me, "cooking" is tossing a slab of raw beef on the grill then standing around with a long skinny fork in one hand and a beer in the other. In fact, I view any meal that doesn't involve animal flesh charred over a gas flame to be a near tragedy – better than starvation, but not all that much.

So you can imagine the panic that gripped me not too long ago when I tried to light my trusty old grill, Carl, and his whole front panel fell off. This resulted in a pretty alarming situation, with gas hissing in the air, the whole front half of Carl hanging there by the gas lines, and me standing right in the middle of the blast zone holding a platter of raw chicken breasts.

This was not the first time Carl had suffered some sort of malfunction. The most interesting incident was the time he broke away from the post he was mounted on, burst into flames and went down like the Hindenburg. Oh, the hamburgers!

For years, after each of the previous Carl mishaps I was able to rally the support of my mechanically-inclined (and hungry) friends to help me patch the old fellow back together. This time, I could see that we had come to the end of the line. As I stood there looking helplessly at the wreckage of my old friend, my wife came out and suggested that I a.) turn off the gas, and b.) go out and buy a new grill.

Have you looked at 21st century barbecue grills? These stainless steel marvels are basically DeLoreans with side-burners.

For you younger people, a DeLorean was a car built in the early 1980s that was basically a stainless steel grill with leather seats.

Of course before I went shopping I did all the necessary consumer research, asking all the important questions: How many burners do I want? Do I need a rotisserie? How does the cooking area compare with the acreage of our typical meal? Will I make it completely over the roof of the house if I forget to open the lid before I light the burners? How much room do I have left on my credit card?

Eventually I found the perfect grill. Of course, it's a bit larger than Carl was, in much the same way an aircraft carrier is a bit larger than a jet ski. Assembling and installing it went pretty well, with only one small bag of parts left over, marked in big red letters, "Critical!!! You must something, something, something before attempting to something, something, something!!!" In the interest of tidiness, I tossed the bag in the trash.

I almost immediately discovered that I don't quite make it over the roof of the house if I forget to open the lid before I light the burners.

And then at last I found myself standing happily with a long skinny fork in one hand and a beer in the other, watching the brand-new flames from my brand new grill engulf a pork chop. The only remaining problem I have is what to name the big guy.

I'm thinking "Enterprise."

Part I: Bikes, Docks & Slush Nuggets

Minuet in G? It's My Wife.

In my opinion, the two greatest inventions of all time are cell phones and those little plastic dealies on the end of shoe laces. Those of you who think I should promote things like penicillin or nuclear power onto this list have obviously never tried to lace a kid's hockey skate with those little plastic dealies missing.

It's hard to estimate the impact cell phones have had on our culture. Why, there are people alive today who have no idea what it would be like to sit in a movie without hearing a high school girl a couple of rows back bellowing, "Of course I love you, Bobby. No, moron, I said, 'I LOVE YOU!'"

Well, I love my cell phone even more than she loves that moron Bobby, and I don't go anywhere without it. I can't imagine not having the ability to instantly tell my friends and family, "You're breaking up. What? Hello?"

My love affair with mobile communication goes clear back to the 1980s, when I carried my portable "bag" phone around in a thing that looked like a vinyl trombone case with an antenna. I took boastful pleasure in calling all my wireless-challenged friends from the golf course and saying things like, "Guess where I'm calling fro... hold on, my battery pack just tipped the golf cart over."

The 2005-model cell phone I'm packing now is about the size of a matchbook, but it contains technology considerably more advanced than the space shuttle. It has a built-in clock and calendar, so I'll always know how late I am in minutes, hours, days or months. I can send text messages with it, replacing the drudgery of a 30-second conversation with half an hour pecking away at the keypad. It even has a camera in it, with a really sensitive trigger, so I'll be able to reminisce for years over my gallery of candid snap shots of car keys and pocket change.

My phone came with more than fifty cool ring tones, enabling me to annoy a moderate-sized crowd with the 1812 Overture rendered by an orchestra of kazoo-playing chipmunks.

The neatest feature is that it's voice-activated. I simply say what I want and the phone does something that more-or-less rhymes. For instance, if I say, "Call home," my phone dials the Vatican.

Of course there are down sides. It's rare these days to see anyone driving a car who isn't holding a cell phone to their ear, and even rarer to see someone who's been in a fender-bender who doesn't have a cell phone stuck up their nose.

Then there are those "Bluetooth" headsets, worn by people who are way too important to hold a phone in their hands. I find it particularly unnerving when a guy I've never seen before walks up wearing a headset, looks me in the eye and says, "Ok Honey, you pick up the kids, and I'll be by to get you at seven-thirty. I love you too. Bye."

Believe it or not, there are still some people who aren't completely comfortable around all this advanced technology. This morning my wife called me from her cell phone;

"Hi," she shouted. How do I get this thing off 'Speaker Phone?'"

"See the little button with a picture of a speaker on it?"

"Yes."

"Push that."

I love being a techie.

A Box 'O Wine And Thou

Living in the tiny town of Whitmore Lake, Michigan is a little bit like scarfing down a whole package of Oreos while you watch a Three Stooges movie – the experience is very pleasant, but you're not necessarily going to brag to all your high-class pals about it.

Now before you start writing me angry letters, I'm not saying that I'm the least bit ashamed of living here. I love living here. I know lots of people who also live here, and I love knowing them. During the months you don't have to thaw the air in a microwave oven before you breathe it, there is not a nicer place to live on the planet.

It's just that when your friend Skyler McSnooty says, "The best thing about our nine-bedroom cottage in Cape Cod is the tennis court we put in for the servants," you're not likely to come back with, "Oh yeah? Well, I'm walking distance from Polly's Market!"

As you can see, Skyler and I live in two completely different worlds. In my world, anything with nine or more bedrooms is either a mansion or a hotel – it is certainly not a "cottage." And while I'm really glad that Skyler wants his butler to have a strong backhand, you have to understand that I'm a lot more concerned with keeping my bread, milk and beer supply lines open.

If you're new to the area, if you're considering moving here, or if you're wondering what the heck you're doing here, I've devised a little quiz to help you determine if you have the right temperament to be a true Whitmore Lakeazoid.

Question 1: When you buy wine, you generally go for;

a.) Something playful yet subtle, hopefully complementing the palate of the entrée; perhaps a Merlot or a Pinot Noir

b.) White Zinfandel

c.) White Zinfandel in a box

d.) The cheapest White Zinfandel in a box

Question 2: Your idea of a night of culture is:

a.) Some Grand Opera, perhaps Mozart's Le nozze de Figaro

b.) A tractor pull

c.) Watching your brother-in-law try to park his motor home in your driveway without taking out the street light

d.) A package of Oreos and a Three Stooges movie

Question 3: What you'd most like to add on to your home is;

a.) A new wing, with a conservatory to accommodate the children's cello and viola lessons.

b.) A new bathroom, with a plaque dedicating it to your daughter

c.) A slab with hook-ups for your brother-in-law's motor home

d.) A six pack and a lawn chair

Question 4: When unexpected guests drop in you;

a.) Whip up a little foie gras, ratatouille over salmon medallions, and maybe a platter of Nicoise olives

b.) Break out the chips and salsa – but only the good salsa

c.) Thaw out the cocktail wieners left over from your son's last birthday party

d.) Get a twelve pack and another lawn chair

If you answered "a.)" to any or all of the above

questions, you would probably not be entirely happy around here. You and the McSnootys can just go live in Hyannis Port, or wherever.

Any other set of answers, and you'll fit in around here just fine.

Moving Out

I fondly remember the day a few years ago when my 21-year-old live-at-home college student son announced happily, "Dad, I've found a great apartment, and I'm moving out." While I knew I was going to miss him, I was glad to have him asserting his independence and leaving home without the assistance of federal marshals.

"So, you want to move out," I said, paternally.

"Hey, you caught on right away," he replied. "And they say old people have a hard time keeping up with new thoughts and ideas!"

"Right. So where is this apartment?"

"Real close to school."

"I see. And who are you rooming with?"

"This guy Tony, who used to work with Tom."

Part I: Bikes, Docks & Slush Nuggets

"Now we're getting some information! And who would Tom be?"

"You know Tom. He was here last New Year's."

"Is he the one who slept under the piano?"

"The bathtub."

"Ah yes, that Tom. Worked with young Tony, did he?"

"In the prison laundry or something."

"So Tony's rehabilitated then?"

"According to the parole board."

And so it went. We learned that Tony was really a good guy, that he had a girlfriend who could cook, and that he had a stereo with butt-kicking speaker columns he bought out of the trunk of a Mazda over by the high school.

Tony's credentials established, we moved on to financial matters;

"So where will you get the money to pay the rent?"

"Well, I'm working four hours a week for $7 per hour."

"Decided against that math major, did you?"

And so we proceeded, carefully discussing and weighing all aspects of the pending move. Eventually we worked our way around to the actual logistical considerations;

"So when are you moving?"

"Tomorrow."

"What will you be taking?"

"I don't know. Some stuff, I guess."

"And how are you going to move everything?"

"We'll get a truck or something."

Thus reassured that all the details had been carefully ironed out, I could relax until moving day rolled around.

I came home the next evening to find the living room couch, the coffee table, and all the furniture from the den missing. I intercepted my son and five of his friends out in the driveway, loading a rusty pickup truck.

"Where are you going with the pool table?"

"Mom said I could take it."

"Do you have room for it in the apartment?"

"I'm pretty sure it'll fit out on the deck."

After five or six trips, the house was pretty much looted and my child was gone. The next evening, I sat alone on the carpet where my favorite chair once was, looking at where the television used to be, and waxing nostalgic over passing one more milestone through the kidneys of my life. Then the phone rang;

"Dad?"

"Hi son! How's the apartment?"

"Great! It turns out there's a party store right next door! And, even with two couches and a coffee table in the living room, there was room for six people to sleep on the floor last night. Say Dad, what does it mean when the smoke detector goes off?"

"It means the place is on fire."

"That's what I thought. (aside) See, I told you dude. It's not a real fireplace. Ok, thanks Dad. Talk to you later. Bye."

"Goodbye son."

Fuzzy Guys

A number of readers have sent emails with comments about the photo of me that runs with this column. First, let me clear up the main point of confusion – I'm the one on the right. The one on the left is Brenna The Dog, who not only thinks she's human, she thinks I'm sending her to Princeton next fall.

We have three cats and Brenna The Dog living in our house right now, which leaves us just about one goat short of a petting zoo. Interestingly, all of our livestock contingent enjoy a similarly elevated view of their position in the overall scheme of things.

This, like pretty much everything around our house, is my fault.

In this space a few weeks ago I mentioned that if something is alive around here, my wife is in

Part I: Bikes, Docks & Slush Nuggets

charge. In the case of the animals, this is because when it comes to anything with fur and sad eyes, I'm a C. P. – a Complete Pushover.

Being a C. P. has its advantages. When I walk into the house, all the animals converge on me like hungry panhandlers. If I've been gone for more than about fifteen minutes, they hold a tickertape parade and present me with the ceremonial Key to the Litter Box.

As much as I'd like to think this adulation reflects their undying esteem for me as a person, I know better. In their eyes I'm really more of a giant Milk Bone and Tuna Snaps dispenser.

This leaves my wife to be the disciplinarian. She's the one who has to say things like, "No! You do not eat Hondas! Bad Dog!" while I stand behind her and silently make conciliatory gestures in Doggie Sign Language. She takes them to the vet and throws the pills down their throats, while I let them lick out the ice cream dishes. She makes them get down from wherever they're not supposed to be up on, and I... well, I don't.

Of course, this inter-species love fest is a two-way street. Brenna The Dog is always willing to snuggle up with me and share the scent of the dead carp she's been rolling in, while the cats are glad to favor me by hocking a hairball into my loafers.

What I've Learned So Far...

One thing I don't understand is how every animal everywhere seems to know that I'm a C. P. All I can figure is that there must have been some sort of feature article about me in the Fuzzy Guys Newsletter. In any case, everywhere I go I'm a magnet for everything from ferrets to a friend's little dog that is basically a cotton ball with cold nose and a tail.

The ultimate expression of my C. P-ness came a few years ago when my son, then about eleven, came home with a puppy that was apparently half Rottweiler and half kangaroo. True to form, I said, "Sure, let's keep... it!" I was already designing a brand-new Beast House by the time my wife came home and sent little Slobbery back to the neighbors who owned the mother - and who had discovered that my son and I actually did just fall off a turnip truck.

It's a good thing somebody's in charge around here.

Does Anyone Make A Hemi In Mauve?

I'm going to go way out on a limb here and make a bold statement:

Men are real different from women!

There, I said it. If this is going to ignite a firestorm of controversy, so be it. I can take the heat. I think.

Now I'm not talking about the kind of differences your little friends used to point out when you were nine years old and trying to figure out why boys and girls use separate bathrooms. I'm talking about some basic differences in the way our brains are wired.

Suppose I were to say, "Hey, I got a new car."

A man will ask, "Did you get the hemi and the towing package?"

A woman will ask, "What color is it?"

Or if I were to ask, "What kind of car are you shopping for?

A man will reply, "A Viagmobile GT. It'll do zero to sixty in 4.8 seconds – equipped with a hemi and a towing package."

A woman will reply, "A blue one."

Let me hasten to add here that I, like every married guy who doesn't want to sleep in the garage tonight, will testify that women are at least as smart as men, and are entirely capable of understanding complex mechanical things. Women make great scientists, engineers, astronauts, world leaders and even combat pilots.

It's just that you know the female wing commander will wind up standing next to her F18 saying, "Yeah, it has a fully integrated weapons system and it does better than Mach 2, but I really wish it came in something a little more interesting than silver."

Of course, women's sensitivity to appearance goes far beyond colors. Before she leaves the house, my wife spends a minimum of an hour making sure every hair is in place and that she doesn't have lipstick on her teeth. She even knows that every article of clothing she's wearing looks good together.

I, on the other hand, go out exactly half the

Part I: Bikes, Docks & Slush Nuggets

time with my sweatshirt on backwards.

I think the most likely explanation for this discrepancy is that in the case of men, our eyes don't seem to completely connect to our brains. How else would you explain tank tops and aloha shirts?

Men actually are theoretically capable of understanding aesthetic concepts. You can explain to me the principles of what looks good and what doesn't, and I'll technically grasp the meaning of every word you say. Then I'll put on my favorite t-shirt – a kind of faded blue number with a mustard-brown "Barefoot International" logo on it, decorated with a gala pattern of ripped seams and moth holes – wink at myself as I walk past the mirror, and head on into town.

See? The eyes and the brain just are not hooking up.

There are a few rudimentary synaptic connections in men's heads, though. For example, we like to keep our cars clean and polished. This is because, like most primates, we are attracted by shiny objects. And we can also see things in motion, which is why we can spot a phantom tag at second base from three hundred feet, but not the way socks, sandals and hairy legs look together.

What I've Learned So Far...

    This, incidentally, is why men can't seem to spot a clump of dirt the size of a Hummer on the living room carpet – dirt doesn't dribble a basketball.

Big Boys and Toys

While we're on the subject of men versus women (We are? Yes, of course we are. If you had paid attention to the previous column, you would know that!) we might as well talk about men and our love affair with toys.

I'll be the first to admit it – most men never really mature much beyond the Roy Rogers pajamas stage, and I am a prime example. I can still remember lying awake at night, wishing I could be outside playing with my new bike – the one with the streamers hanging from the ends of the handlebars and the playing cards flapping in the spokes.

Of course, over the years the objects of my toy lust have evolved. For one thing, I still have a bike I dream of riding, but I no longer have playing cards in the spokes.

What I've Learned So Far...

No comment on those streamers.

This evolution means that many of the things I now covet as toys tend to be at least allegedly useful. You can attribute this to the fact that my toy fetish is centered in the "Cool Tool Gene" that I have mentioned from time to time.

In other words, men are genetically programmed to say things like, "I need that reciprocating saw, Honey. The one I have doesn't even begin to reciprocate, and you of all people should know just how frustrating something like that can be!"

Women are different. Lacking the Cool Tool Gene, a woman will never buy a piece of hardware unless she actually has some kind of use for it. For example, let's say a woman has a nail that she wants to drive into a wall. If she can't pound that nail in with her cell phone or with the side of the TV remote, and she can't borrow a hammer from the neighbors, she may break down and buy one.

A guy, on the other hand, will survey the situation and question whether a nail has the holding power to really do the job. Then he will go out and spend $150 on a power drill, $35 on a complete set of drill bits, and $28 on a box of 1,000 #6 1 1/2" pan head screws. Then he'll spend weeks searching for somewhere to use the other 999 #6 1 1/2" pan head screws.

Part I: Bikes, Docks & Slush Nuggets

Of course, as indifferent as a woman is to tools, she can get all tingly over a dress, a pair of shoes and matching purse. She can focus her whole existence on a quest to find a little black skirt that's just a smidgen shorter/longer/blacker than any of the little black dresses she already has. That's right, incredible as it may seem, my wife feels pretty much the same way about all the crap in her closet as I do about my new weed whacker!

So it's a pretty safe bet that you'll never hear any man call his buddy and say, "Phil, you have just got to see the new steel-toed boots I found! They match my tool belt perfectly – and they were on sale!" But thanks to the Cool Tool Gene, if a guy gets a new riding mower, he'll notify the media and issue a press release.

Predictably, there is a scientific explanation for women's strange indifference to tools. I have it on good authority that instead of the Cool Tool Gene, women have a thing called the Craving Clothing Chromosome. There are big words involved, so it must be true.

But we'll talk a little more about that in a future column.

Big Boys and Big Toys

Last week we talked about big boys and their toys. I'm sure most women were just stunned to learn that, when it comes to their stuff, most guys are emotionally about eight years old. Now we'll move on and discuss the most important material thing in the average man's life:

The curtains in the guest bathroom!

No, wait, that's not right. I'm pretty sure the average man would have a hard time telling you whether or not he even had a guest bathroom, unless he had recently replaced the toilet in there. What I really meant to say was:

His car!

Yeah, that's better. There's no question about it, we men have a thing for our cars. I think this might be because driving our cars is about the only time in our lives we have any control at all over what's going on.

Think about it. When we were kids, our moms and other women - grandmothers, babysitters and teachers - were in charge of where we went, what we did, and how we did it pretty much every waking minute. The most common thing we heard from our fathers was, "I don't know. You'd better go ask your mother."

As we began to grow up, the ladies temporarily handed the controls off to our girlfriends – "Go ahead and take him out for a test-drive, dear, but don't let him get away from you on the curves." And later our mothers were proud and happy to sign the title and registration over to our new wives – "If you just keep his tank full and change his oil now and then, he won't give you any trouble."

But when we get behind the wheel of our cars, we are in charge. Top dog. Numero uno! The big cheese! That car is going to go where we tell it to go!

Unless, of course, a wife or girlfriend has somewhere she wants us to take her...

Now one thing that you women might have noticed about men is that we like to take care of our cars. The same guy who can never seem to find the laundry hamper with his boxer shorts can spend an hour polishing a squashed bug off his fender. I actually have a friend who cleans the brake dust from his hub caps with a tooth brush. To his credit, he is always careful to rinse that toothbrush well before he puts it back in his wife's medicine cabinet.

As for me, I might fail to notice a dust ball the size of a dead buffalo in the living room, but a gum wrapper on my passenger-side floor mat sends me into a cleaning frenzy.

Now a man also needs to get himself the right kind of car. After all, there are "girl cars" and there are "guy cars," and no self-respecting man would be caught dead driving a "girl car."

Except me. I just can't seem to get the hang of the whole "girl car / guy car" thing. During my adult life I've owned a Buick, a Volkswagen, a Porsche, a Cadillac, a Volvo, a Jeep, and a PT Cruiser. Within a week of buying every one of these, I've had a friend say to me, "Yeah, that's a real nice car. I just bought one for my daughter, and the turbocharged model with the bigger engine than the one you got for my wife."

So there you have it. The secret's out – guys just don't care about curtains! Next week maybe we'll talk a little bit about "girl cars."

Girl Cars

Last week on this page we talked about guys and their obsession with the automobile. In the course of that discussion I happened to mention "girl cars." As you might have guessed, this sparked a bit of controversy and some letters from readers;

Dear Mr. Funny Guy,

You got a lot of nerve! Why I ought to rip your arm off and beat you with the bloody stump, you no good commie...

Yours truly, your biggest fan,

Sister Mary Catherine

Well Sister, I sure didn't mean to offend you or any of the other chicks who read my column. Mea culpa! Ha, ha, ha.

It's just that men and women truly do have different attitudes toward cars. Women use them to get where they want to go. Men build shrines around them.

Not that women aren't picky about what they drive. When they go car shopping they consider "important factors" like styling, color, comfort, and utility – how adorable is that! Women will almost never base their decision on really critical issues like the bench horsepower of the model their pal Toby just bought.

"But what about Danica Patrick?" you ask. Ok, maybe you didn't ask that, but play along with me here.

Danica Patrick almost won the Indianapolis 500, finished fourth, and was named 2005 Rookie Of The Year. She's become a major force in the Indy Racing League and appears to be headed for a career as maybe one of the best open-wheel race drivers of all time. So what kind of car does she drive?

A Honda. Now we all know that Hondas are good on gas and practical for getting around the track, all things considered. Danica just drives her Honda really, really fast.

Ok, I'll admit that I'm a major Danica Patrick fan. She's talented, intelligent, articulate, attractive, and I can tell just by looking at her that she would be nice enough to push the seat back when she gets out of that race car so the next guy that comes along doesn't bash his knees into hamburger trying to get in.

Ladies please take note of this last point. If you would consider leaving the car seat pushed back so that anyone taller than a Keebler Elf can get behind the wheel, you might just get us guys to start putting the toilet seat down.

Here's an interesting thing I noticed – Danica Patrick doesn't seem to wear much in the way of makeup. This might be partly because she doesn't really need much, but I think it might also reflect the relative difficulty of putting on eye liner at 225 miles per hour. That, and there's no center rear-view "makeup mirror" in an Indy car.

Anyway, I've decided that the main thing that identifies a true "girl car" might not be so much what kind of car it is, but how it gets used – usually as a sort of rolling long-term storage facility. Most men don't even want to keep a car as long as a woman will haul around a stack of old magazines or a tote bag full of used tennis balls.

And this brings us to the question of the day – do you think Danica keeps a dozen chipped flower pots and a box headed for the Salvation Army in the trunk of that Honda?

Great Column Ideas

People often ask me, "Where do you get the ideas for your columns?" Then they go on to say things like, "Why, you must be some kind of genius to come up with such great material week after week!" Or, "Why, you're so clever, you should run for Emperor of the World!"

Ok, nobody's ever said any of that other stuff.

But to answer the question, my ideas come from lots of places. First, unusual things are always happening to me. This is probably because I get myself into a lot of unusual situations. I mean, anyone who knows full well that he is a charter member of the, "...never let this guy play with machinery or pointy objects..." club, and yet naively attempts to sharpen the lawn mower, can pretty much count on an adventure in his near future.

Part I: Bikes, Docks & Slush Nuggets

Reading the news can also be a rich source of material, so I try to stay alert for interesting things going on in the world. For instance, I recently read that the government on Prince Edward Island has decided to cut back the operating hours of their suicide hotline. This means that anyone calling after 5:00 PM will get a message telling them to call back during normal business hours. Or they can, presumably, leave a note...

And there was the recent World Toilet Expo, which had all of Shanghai, China flushed with excitement.

Sorry about that.

But the real key to turning a mishap involving a barbecue grill, a saucepan of gravy, and a small natural gas explosion into the sort of fine literature you see here, is keeping copious notes. I try to write everything down, hopefully even before the gravy re-enters the atmosphere. Everywhere I go I have scratch pads, 3x5 cards, post-its, old envelopes and napkins covered with my brainstorms. I just can't risk losing the inspiration that someday I really should do a piece on dog poo.

My most entertaining notebook is the one I keep next to the bed, in which I document all the brilliant insights that wake me from a sound sleep at three in the morning. These pages have yielded several columns, a chapter in a novel, and a short story that may become a novel.

Unfortunately my penmanship, not all that good under the best of conditions, is even worse performed in a dark room when I've apparently forgotten which hand I normally write with. This has produced some fairly puzzling entries like;

Write a barimmen about how every florbet has vleb sneeves. Especially when you consider the florbet's seven little plevers. It Will Be Hilarious!

This epiphany is followed on the page by a diagram of some sort of animal in a top hat standing on what looks like a large casserole dish.

I have to admit, though, that sometimes notes that I can read are not all that much easier to understand. Here's a recent entry – verbatim;

Walking home from a party, falling through the ice near the edge of a shallow pond by the high school / college while wife is trying to distract and annoy the tuba player practicing inside.

Now that I think of it, and at the risk of annoying tuba players everywhere, that just may be the subject of a future column...

Part I: Bikes, Docks & Slush Nuggets

The Fourth of July

Well, here it is – the Fourth of July Weekend! All across the United States something like 286 million bags of crushed ice are heading for coolers, and a similar number of Americans are heading for any place featuring sunshine and other Americans. We're going to celebrate our nation's independence.

Most of us know about how our country was founded on the inalienable right to eat brats and play Frisbee on a weekday in July. In the interest of our long-term success as a lawn-party nation, I thought we would take a few minutes and go over some of the finer points of the Big Day.

Hamburgers: These are an essential part of any Fourth of July celebration. The perfect burgers should be cooked over a charcoal fire that is just slightly cooler than the surface of the sun. You will know that they are bun-ready when they resemble little flat lumps of charcoal.

Hot Dogs: These get cooked over the same fire as the hamburgers, but not for quite as long. Hot dogs have no nutritional value at all, but they team up with their buns to serve as pretty good delivery vehicles for horseradish and mustard. They are also around to make the hamburgers seem like food by comparison.

Watermelon: I can't think of anything better on a hot day. Cut it nice and thick, so you can't eat it without getting juice all over your shirt and up your nose. If you're over the age of about twelve, you should probably avoid seed-spitting contests.

Potato Salad: Of course it's good for you. Why else would they call it "salad?"

Sunscreen: Be sure you slather on plenty of sunscreen. This is especially important when your son waits until you fall asleep in the sun, then writes "Loser" on your back with SPF 60.

Aloe: For any spots you missed with the sunscreen. If you overlooked the note above, that's everything except the word "Loser" on your back.

Fireworks: I love watching fireworks, but I leave the actual detonation of them to professionals and self-destructive pyromaniacs.

Part I: Bikes, Docks & Slush Nuggets

I once bought one of those huge boxes of "Legal Fireworks" at the grocery store. The colorful packaging suggested that I would have enough "Safe, Legal" firepower in there to put on a thirty minute show over the Statue of Liberty.

When I opened it up at home, my arsenal consisted mostly of a variety of plastic gizmos that made puffs of smoke and little farting sounds. The most exciting "Safe, Legal" pyrotechnics we got were sparklers.

I burned my foot stepping on a sparkler.

The Parade: You can't celebrate the Fourth without watching your friends and neighbors line up and march down Main Street. Better yet, march along with them. Just try not to follow the horses.

The Flag: The American flag is unique in the world. Contrary to the assertions of some folks these days, our flag does not stand for any one political party or point of view. It stands for the rich diversity of opinions, religions, races, and cultural backgrounds that have been forged into an alloy of liberty that is stronger than any metal. And it stands for the countless valiant people who since July 4, 1776 have fought and died to preserve that diversity.

God really does bless America.

Confessions of a Doberman Dad

As I mentioned in this column a few weeks ago, I have a Doberman named Brenna, who happens to be the biggest baby of all dogs.

Ok, I know what you're going to say; that your little poodlie-cocka-whatever is the definition of a cute dog, and that the Doberman Pinscher is big and vicious.

Yeah, right.

True enough, Dobies were originally bred for military use, police work, and Disney movies. Their hair is short and their ears are cropped so they won't get caught in barbed wire while infiltrating enemy lines. Their tails are cropped so they won't wag them and knock over a lamp while infiltrating the living room.

The Doberman has many advantages over other dogs. They are exactly as tall as your dining

Part I: Bikes, Docks & Slush Nuggets

table, so they are always in perfect position to snatch your pork chop or knock the bowl of mashed potatoes into the lap of your dinner guest. They are strong enough to wedge their noses under your hand and flip your glass of Chablis into the next room.

They have powerful shoulders and hind quarters, giving them speed, agility and the ability to back smoothly up onto your lap when you're seated in an ordinary arm chair. Dobies lack the back-up "beeper" you hear on most public works vehicles, but I understand scientists are working on this by cross-breeding them with garbage trucks.

The name "Brenna" is Gaelic for "I'm a huge pansy and I have no clue how scary I look." She "grins" when she greets people, baring her teeth and shaking her head from side to side. She is not aware that this makes her look a little like the Alien licking his chops over Sigourney Weaver in a sweaty tank top. We adopted Brenna from Doberman Rescue as a two-year-old – which is, along with the Humane Society, the very best way to get a dog of any breed.

The first weekend we had Brenna living with us, a female friend wandered into the kitchen in search of peanut butter, unaware that the house was now protected against just that sort of dangerous intrusion. My friend and my dog met and surprised each other somewhere between the blender and the microwave.

Did you know that many females, both human and canine, have bladder-control problems when they're surprised?

Not long after what is now known throughout these parts as the Tandem-Tinkle Incident, Brenna surrounded and captured a juvenile duck down by the lake. I was horrified speechless at the sight of the poor little duck, its neck swinging limp as Brenna trotted proudly toward us. Fortunately, my wife had the presence of mind to say, "Brenna! Spit that out," to which Brenna replied, "Ptui!"

As Brenna and the rest of us watched, the duck hopped up and strolled away without a scratch, doubtless to tell his duck buddies all about his brush with those grinning Jaws of Death and to write the screenplay for a Disney movie about a mean Doberman.

So there you have it – the Doberman's terrifying reputation is not really deserved. I have to admit, though, that it's sometimes kind of fun to have a dog who can greet the thirty-year-old guy, standing at the front door wearing a grimy name badge and selling magazine subscriptions to win the Teen Entrepreneurs' Trip to Europe, and with one "WOOF" make him reevaluate his career choice.

Modern Communication

I just read about a couple in India who got married by cell phone, because the groom got caught in a monsoon and couldn't make it through the flood waters to get to the wedding.

Wow! Talk about blowing away that last really great excuse! After this, those of you who thought you were going to fall back on the old "Honey, I tried to make it home in time to go to the third grade clarinet recital, but a monsoon washed the road out!" story will have to come up with something new.

I wonder how fifteen out-of-tune clarinets would sound over a cell phone?

Admittedly, that little lump of technology in your pocket or purse can keep you within striking range of just about every variety of nagging and harassment. But try not to get too down on the little guy – it also opens up a whole world of possibilities. For one thing, your cell phone is an invaluable safety tool. It lets you immediately call for help if you've broken down on the highway, or for your spouse if you become separated in the Discount Club store.

And then there is my friend who uses his cell phone and a sound effects tape in his car to orchestrate excuses for every occasion. Through the magic of electronics, he can sit in the lot at the golf course and call his boss from a traffic jam, the emergency room, an airport ticket counter, or the examination room of a spaceship bound for the Crab Nebula; "They're probing me – nooooooooo!"

If you do this though, be very careful not to record your sounds over a used tape. My friend had a hard time explaining to his wife why Gwen Stefani suddenly started singing during the "prayer service" that was going on in his Buick parked outside the tavern.

Of course, there will be times when you don't want to be at the mercy of your cell phone. For those of you who would like to learn to live with or even get the upper hand on your little electronic pal, there are a lot of things you can do that are a little more creative than turning the thing off and not knowing how to retrieve your voice mail.

First, there's the "Gosh, I must have dropped the cell or something!" gambit. This one is best used on people who just haven't figured out that the conversation pretty much ended about ten minutes ago. The key to success here is to start a sentence; "Oh, I almost forgot to tell you about the grzzzzznxxxxt..." And then turn off the power.

Of course there are almost endless variations you can use. The real secret is to master an assortment of "static" noises.

Then there's the "I'll have to call you back – I'm getting into heavy traffic – AAAAAaaaarghhhhh!" routine. This one is good when you just didn't look closely enough at the caller ID before you answered the call. Later, you can tell your caller all about the near miss you had while you were talking to them.

Come to think of it, wouldn't a "near miss" essentially be a "hit?"

Finally, there's the "I have to hang up now because I've reached the front of the line at the bank, and the cashier just handed me a threatening note!" ploy.

Hey! How about just hanging up before you go into the bank?

Nah.

Life In A Cat House

A couple of weeks ago I wrote about Brenna the Dog, the big scary Doberman in our family who is actually a giant cream puff with fuzzy ears. Now I've been asked to provide equal time for our cats. Ok, here goes.

First off, I'm pretty sure we have three cats. I'm not completely sure, because you can never be completely sure of anything when it comes to cats. I have my suspicions that one of them might be a really tiny covert federal agent in a kitty suit, but so far Karl Rove has been uncharacteristically silent on the subject.

All three of the cats we have right now are female. Since they have all been "fixed," this was really only important when it came to naming them: "Muffin," a.k.a. "Muffer;" "Libby," a.k.a.

"The Phantom;" and Mindy," a.k.a. "I'm Not Fat, I'm Just Fluffy."

Until a year ago we also had a more-or-less-male cat named "Benny." As near as we could tell, he was an expert in antiques and had a bit of a flair for interior design. Benny was so in touch with his feminine side that he was also known as "Esmeralda." Last summer the little guy went to that great Versace scratching post in the sky, and we miss him a lot.

Our cats divide their days into two major sections. First is the "Sleeping Time" which lasts roughly twenty-two hours per day. Through careful observation, we've been able to identify a number of different sleeping modes. These include "snoozing," "napping," "slumbering," "just resting my eyes," "zonked," "dead to the world," and "crapped out on top of the refrigerator."

If you should happen to need a cat during the Sleeping Time (ok, nobody in history has ever actually "needed a cat," but just play along with me here) all you have to do is fire up the can opener.

The balance of a cat's life is the "Mostly Not Sleeping Time," which is divided into twelve periods of around ten minutes each, scattered throughout the day and night. Typical Mostly Not Sleeping Time activities include staring at a spider on a window, stomping across your pillow at 4 AM, carrying a stuffed mouse around and yowling, staring at a window with no spider on it, and scouting for a good place to catch a little shuteye.

If you should happen to catch up with a cat during the Mostly Not Sleeping Time and scratch her belly, she will immediately punch out and head back for the Sleeping Time.

You would think that with three cats in the house, we'd be pretty much free of mice. You would be right. We had a family of mice move in earlier this summer, apparently planning a nice vacation on the lake, but it didn't really work out for them. If you don't mind, I'd rather not dwell on the details.

So there you have it. Despite my being, as I admitted a few weeks ago, a C.P. (Complete Pushover) for animals, my wife has managed to limit our menagerie to cats and dogs. We've passed on gerbils, ferrets, snakes, hamsters, toads, rabbits, tarantulas, degus, skinks, more snakes, parakeets, condors, llamas, and Gila monsters.

Come to think of it, my wife might be out of town for a couple of days next month. Anybody know where I can adopt a nice baby otter?

If I Only Had A Bike

Ok, I realize that I write a lot about the differences between men and women. That's because there are just so many differences, and most of them are a lot of fun to write about. So get over it.

For instance, the other day I happened to overhear four kids, two boys and two girls, all in about the fifth grade, exchanging fairly typical ten-year-old-kid banter. Suddenly one of the boys shouted at one of the girls, in that universal taunting sing-song that seems to have been genetically hard-wired into every child in the history of the world, "You don't have a peee-nis!"

Without missing a beat, the little girl replied, "Oh yeah? Well, you don't have a bike!"

And there we have it – a perfect illustration of the fundamental gap in priorities between the male and female of our species. And guys, I hate to break it to you, but the girls are way out ahead of us.

You see, men have a pathological tendency to get distracted by things that are completely irrelevant to the situation at hand, while women are more prone to stay focused on the things that matter – like their ride home. For adults, who would presumably have moved beyond chanting about who has what body parts, an obvious example of this might be Sports Fandom. Women can apparently enjoy watching a game, then move on to things that actually affect their lives.

Weird, huh?

Men, on the other hand, feel the need to embrace any sport they watch in pretty much the same way they approach a foot-long chili cheese dog – with a whole lot more enthusiasm than it probably deserves.

To illustrate the point, my wife and I are both passionate hockey fans, but she can usually go right to sleep after our team drops a big game. As for me, I'm still pretty upset about the Red Wings trading away Adam Oates for Bernie Federko back in 1989. And don't even get me started on the Tigers and Kyle Farnsworth!

And then there's the actual playing of sports. I have a female friend who likes to play ice hockey.

Part I: Bikes, Docks & Slush Nuggets

She likes it a lot. When she's on the ice she throws her heart and soul into the game and skates like crazy. When the game is over, she touches up her makeup and gets on with her life.

When I skated in a men's hockey league a few years ago, you'd have thought I was playing for an NHL contract extension. I was stupid enough to lay down (I went down on purpose – really I did!) in front of slap shots. I would beat myself to a bruised pulp trying to keep up with bigger, faster, younger, stronger players. I'd try not to limp too much when we headed to our cars after the game, because I didn't want the guys to think I was some kind of pansy.

And if my wife was still awake when I dragged my groaning carcass into the house, she would simply smile, shake her head, then head off to do something useful.

Which brings us – somehow – to our kids and how they approach sports. Next week, we'll talk a bit about youth ice hockey.

An Ice Hockey Primer

All the time my son was growing up I coached his ice hockey teams. This means that I spent years standing around ice rinks, plotting complex strategies and line combinations so we could get the drop on enemies like Linda's Craft Center Penguins.

Now most hockey parents know the game, and they can locate a rink from over a mile away just by the smell of Zamboni fumes. For the rest of you, here's a primer on youth ice hockey in North America.

In hockey, we have clever names for each age group. When they first start out, we call them "Mini-Mites," then "Mites." In about the fourth grade they graduate out of the personal parasite class, to become "Squirts," then "Pee Wees." After that we call them "Bantams" for a couple of years, just so we can give them a shred of self-esteem while they go through puberty.

In high school, when they stand six feet or taller in skates, we repeal that tiny shred of dignity and call them "Midgets."

Wherever there are programs for children younger than "Mini-Mites," we call them "Atoms," the name-inventing guys having completely overlooked bacteria and viruses.

Ice hockey is played with "pucks" and "sticks." Pucks are small hard rubber discs, designed to elude anything made of wood. Sticks are made of wood.

We give these sticks to the children, whose idea of fun would pretty much be hitting other children with sticks, then we penalize them for doing that. This confuses them, which builds character.

"Checking" is a little-understood part of the game, not to be confused with "Giving The Manager A Check," which every hockey parent thoroughly understands. Basically, checking consists of the player gliding across the ice, then crushing another player into the boards. The kids enjoy this because it makes a lot of noise and scares their mothers.

We don't allow them to check until they are about eleven years old, so they will have more permanent teeth to knock loose.

At each end of the ice there is a "net" or "goal." Each team has a player called the "goalie," whose job is to stand in front of the net and get hit by the puck. Occasionally a team will "score a goal," which consists of players raising their arms and skating around in wild celebration if the puck happens to miss the goalie and roll into the net. The team who celebrates the most is declared the winner, and the other team files a protest.

The "officials" skate around wearing striped shirts and blowing whistles. Their job is to enforce "the rules," which were made up by "Canadians." Making up these rules apparently involved drinking a great deal of "Molson," because there are a lot of things about hockey, like "Icing the Puck," that nobody can really explain.

A hockey game is divided into three "periods," making it just about impossible to have a "halftime show." This actually works out pretty well in the long run, since a marching band would probably just keep falling down on the ice.

The "other team" is made up of children roughly the size and temperament of a combat Marine battalion masquerading as third graders. Their flagrantly criminal behavior during the game is somehow never detected by the officials, despite the fact that their many transgressions

Part I: Bikes, Docks & Slush Nuggets

are helpfully and constantly pointed out by your team's alert parents.

After the game, the players from both teams are usually laughing and swapping wedgies before they have their skates off, while the parents are discussing class-action lawsuits.

People sometimes ask me if trudging through all those ice-covered parking lots outside the practice rink three hours before dawn, in the middle of winter, with my son asleep over one shoulder and a bag of tiny pads and skates over the other, was worth it.

Yep.

On Plumbing

Not too long ago some plumbing broke in our house. This came to my attention when somebody flushed the toilet upstairs and the ceiling in the basement family room crashed down onto one of the cats.

After giving the cat a bath and a mild sedative, my first impulse was to set up some colored spotlights, designate the area an Ornamental Fountain, then sell the house.

It turns out my wife wasn't quite ready to sell, leaving me with the options of either never using any of the bathrooms again, or fixing the pipe. We also had a plugged-up drain in the upstairs bathtub, so I got in the Yellow Pages to find a plumber.

The first guy I reached said he could get to us sometime in November, 2015. The second one could come over in two weeks, but he wanted an immediate cash deposit that would cover his next 18 Mercedes payments.

I finally found a small ad for "Kevin the Plumer," and rationalized that skill with pipes probably didn't have all that much to do with spelling. As luck would have it, Kevin had some time on his hands, and he didn't require a deposit, so we agreed that he would "stop on over."

Kevin showed up in a pickup truck that was pretty much held together by the dirt caked on it. An apparently random collection of rusty tools, connectors, wire, ladders, brackets and bits of pipe had bounced around in the truck's bed for years, fusing into a sort of grimy abstract sculpture.

Kevin himself was well-matched with the truck, wearing a brown quilted jacket, stained by years of contact with unthinkable substances, and the name "Alvin" inexplicably sewn on the front. He carried a plunger and a small sledgehammer.

Kevin started with the bathtub. He considered the clogged drain thoughtfully in silence for a few seconds, then attacked it violently with the plunger, spraying the bathroom walls and ceiling with black sludge. He had just picked up the sledgehammer and was gazing at the porcelain tub with the hungry look of a crow eyeing road kill, when I stopped him, handed him a $50 bill and thanked him for coming by.

Shaken by my experience with Kevin, I decided to do it myself, with help from my friend Paul. Paul is not a plumber, but he has lots of cool tools, and he knows what most of them are for.

A few days later Paul showed up with new parts and a fairly comprehensive selection of those cool tools. We quickly established a working rhythm, Paul whaling away at the pipe, and me slapping wrenches, pipes, brackets, connectors, or beverages into Paul's hand as he needed them.

The job actually went fairly smoothly, aside from accidentally severing the phone lines. And blowing out the electricity. And cutting a couple of load-supporting ceiling joists. And that one little fire. And, of course, what we now laughingly prefer to call the "pipe-clamp mishap."

In any case, we eventually got everything installed, spliced, reinforced, extinguished, bandaged, and cleaned up.

So if you are ever faced with a similar situation, and you are not yourself a plumber, I advise you to:

1. become a plumber;

2. buy some colored lights, then call the realtor; or

3. get to know Paul.

My Grass Is Never Greener

Ok, I'd just like to know who made it a law that a perfect lawn of rich green grass is good, and all that crap that actually wants to grow out there in your yard is bad.

First, a little background: I bought my house from a retired gentleman whose sole mission in life was to make sure that no blade of grass in the lawn was ever longer or shorter than any other. He was a compulsive grass guy. As a result, on the day we moved in I had the most beautiful yard anybody had ever seen.

Within a week feral cats stalked their prey in my crabgrass Serengeti. Down by the lake, waves of golden dandelions swayed gently in the breeze. A large section of the front yard looked more like the Baja peninsula than anything I've ever seen in

Michigan – my son claimed he spotted a vulture sitting on a cactus over by the porch.

So how did this happen? How did the word get out to all the weeds and varmints that the old sheriff was gone and the new one didn't know his Weed 'N Feed from his 2-4-D?

All I can figure is that there is some sort of botanical underworld organization for chickweed, plantain, and all the other plants deemed "outlaws" by the Code of the Suburbs. And, like good gangsters everywhere, they moved in and took over the minute the territory opened up.

For a while I tried to be a kind of lawn-care Eliot Ness, slinging my spot-weed-eradicator bottle like a Tommy gun, ruthlessly hunting down and blasting everything that wasn't good old law-abiding Kentucky Blue Grass. While this was pretty satisfying in a Dirty Harry kind of way, it wasn't all that effective – for every offender I'd "rub out," two more would spring up in its place.

So maybe it is now time for us to work on repealing this botanical version of the Volstead Act. I once saw a house in Las Vegas, where watering can present a problem, in which the occupant had paved the yard with concrete and painted it a more or less grass-like green color. This individual was clearly capable of thinking outside the box. Why shouldn't the rest of us?

First, why can't I have a lawn made up entirely of Creeping Charlie? It's green, and you never have to mow the stuff. Plus, I'm pretty sure there's nothing short of a nuclear blast that will kill it. The only down side I can think of is that Creeping Charlie smells like mint, so it might be kind of like living on a giant Tic Tac.

Could be worse.

And who says you shouldn't cultivate a prize-winning dandelion patch? You could go to dandelion shows and have dandelion home tours, where people go around and gawk at the very best dandelion gardens in town. You could have little bouquets of dandelions on the table, in stunning arrangements garnished with sprigs of thistle and ragweed.

You could even get out of trouble with your wife by sending her a dozen long-stemmed dandelions. As long as you also sent her a diamond bracelet.

Ok, maybe all that is not such a great idea after all. I wonder what Astroturf costs these days?

Spl Chkr Blooz

Hey, I have an idea. Let's completely redesign the English language.

First a little background. Earlier in my career as a writer, sandwiched in between the days of chiseling my prose into the walls of King Tut's Tomb and working on my PowerBook, I did all my writing on a thing called a "typewriter."

Back in those days, writers had to have at least a vague idea how to spell the words we wanted to use. And if we screwed up, we had to try to spot the problem ourselves. We sometimes even had to "look up" words in a "book" called a "dictionary!"

Booooooring!

These days, whenever I hammer out a piece on my computer, the word processor's spell-checker does a lot of the heavy lifting for me. All I have to do is get within a few electrons of a real word,

Part I: Bikes, Docks & Slush Nuggets

and the computer will correct me or give me suggestions that are programmed right into the software, based on similar mistakes made by a scientifically selected panel of other morons.

Unfortunately, a guy like me who types with his elbows can easily slip right past my computer's little electronic genius with a sentence like, "Lettuce go to the beech to sea same friends!" They're all words – just not quite the ones I had in mind.

Some people have suggested that we should improve spell-checkers to the point where they can analyze and correctly interpret the context of what you're writing. I'm not even entirely sure what that means, much less how it would work.

Instead, I propose that we change the English language to bring it in line with spell-checkers. For instance, we can get rid of problems like "it's" and "its" by simply getting rid of apostrophes. You could just write, "The dog is very happy; its licking its..." whatever it is he happens to be licking.

Likewise, you can get rid of your you're issues, just like they can resolve their they're problems. Over there.

Got that?

This wouldn't be the first time our language got itself updated. Four hundred years ago, a teenager might stick a quill in the old quill-sharpener and dash off a note like this to a friend:

Soft, sweet companion, know that as beloved friend do I love thee in return, and I would that thy visage light up this house, gracing this week's end, dismal in every aspect without thee. Hearken thou hence after two of 't afternoon, for my mother deemest that I must practiceth my clarinet first... eth.

These days, a kid would handle that whole transaction in a text message:

CM OVR THS WKND FTR 2.

To which the friend might craft a heartfelt reply:

K

All right, maybe it's not exactly a sonnet, but it gets the job done.

To get this whole thing started, I propose that we form a group called the Bureau Of Nearly Everybody Hacking English Down, or BONEHED. As a brotherhood and sisterhood of BONEHEDs, we can work together to bring our language at last into the twenty-first century.

So snd mi n email tday n syn up. Wi cn strt bi splng wrds lik thy snd n wthot al ths xtra ltrs!

And whatever you do, weep not for English – you can bet it ain't weeping for you.

Beaucoup Sad

It was a muggy afternoon in New Orleans. I was twenty-five years old, sitting in a bar on Bourbon Street, next to a screenless window that opened to the sidewalk outside. Somewhere in one of the neighboring bars, a trumpet, a clarinet and a tuba carried on a musical dogfight around the melody of some gospel song.

My friend and I had a pile of iced crabs on the table between us, and I was banging on the shell of one with the blunt end of a butter knife. My friend was holding another one up to the light, apparently looking for some sort of pull-tab on the little critter.

A tiny immaculate grey-haired man dressed in a clean but very well-worn black cutaway suit, with a grey vest and a carnation in his lapel, stopped on the sidewalk next to us. "Pardon me sir," he drawled, "but there is a particular technique to that. Would you permit me to demonstrate?"

Then, still standing out on the sidewalk and leaning through the window, he showed us how to elegantly disassemble and eat a fresh Louisiana blue crab, along with a gentle lecture on proper application of lemon and cayenne pepper sauce. When we invited him to come inside and join us for a drink and more crabs, he smiled, bowed slightly, and said, "Alas, I am required elsewhere. But do enjoy your visit to our city."

I wonder where that wonderful little man is now.

New Orleans is not like any other place I've ever been. In that single ordinary weekday afternoon and evening I saw my first Dixieland jazz band, hooker, Creole funeral, street-gutter drunk, antebellum mansion, transvestite – and iced Louisiana blue crab.

In New Orleans I first heard someone speaking Cajun, that verbal gumbo of French, English, Spanish, African, Choctaw, and maybe a little Martian. I listened to barkers on the street delivering impassioned sales pitches for jazz joints, and strip joints, and a few jazz-strip joints.

I walked down streets that had been used

Part I: Bikes, Docks & Slush Nuggets

by general Andrew Jackson and Jean Lafitte the pirate. I stood in a square where slaves had been bought and sold. I sat in a tavern where Lafitte and Jackson may have shared a pint and I heard Al Hirt do things with a trumpet that were not humanly possible. I wandered through a city founded on a sort of unashamed decadence that would probably take several lifetimes to understand.

I wonder where that nasty-wonderful little city is now.

Last week I watched a group of overfed white men on television, standing in a hanger in Mississippi with their shirtsleeves symbolically rolled up to indicate that they were working hard, as they staged a "situational briefing" for the cameras. They told each other things that anyone who could read a newspaper had known for days, and congratulated each other on the wonderful job they were doing.

At that moment in New Orleans more than 50,000 trapped and helpless people had been waiting for days to be rescued. The bodies of drowning victims floated down streets and decomposed in the attics that had been their last refuge in their inundated homes. Some of these people are probably descendants of the slaves that were traded in the streets of the French Quarter 170 years ago. Virtually all of them are among the poorest people living anywhere in the richest nation the world has ever known.

Cut off by the floods and not having worked their way up in the hierarchy of priorities held by the leaders of our nation – who needed a couple of days to wrap up their vacations and plan their photo-ops before sending help – these people lived through the nightmare of an almost total collapse of civilization. They watched helplessly as the oldest and the youngest and the sickest among them died. They watched a few morally bankrupt young men, armed with looted guns and liquor, carry out a reign of terror unchecked by the handful of police officers left in the city.

I guess New Orleans will be drained and rebuilt some day. Eventually the French Quarter will sputter back to life, and the musicians, and the blue crabs, and the strippers will all resurface to take their places on Bourbon Street.

But I wonder if New Orleans will ever regain that sense of innocent debauchery that would allow an old man with a carnation in his lapel to lean through a window to give a young man a lesson in Bayou dining.

God, I hope so.

Part I: Bikes, Docks & Slush Nuggets

Confessions of a Kamikaze Athlete

It was just after a session of sunset barefooting, and two of my friends were carrying my shattered body up the dock from the lake. My wife was standing on the shore with her hands on her hips in that universal wife-pose that clearly says, "All right, Einstein, what happened this time?"

I simply smiled bravely and said, "Aaaaaaarrrrrggghhhhhh."

In an attempt to flesh out my explanation, one of my buddies told her, "Sorry. We broke your husband." On the up side, I didn't actually fracture my hip, as the doctor had thought at first.

I'm willing to admit that I sometimes make questionable athletic decisions. And while I rarely make the same mistake twice, I have lived long and enthusiastically enough to make plenty of mistakes the first time.

As a result, the receptionist at the physical therapy clinic has my Blue Cross number memorized, and they keep a coffee mug with my name on it in their break room. Over the years, these teams of dedicated professionals have helped me fight my way back to a productive life after dislocations, strained muscles, compression fractures, torn ligaments, crushed fingers, concussions, contusions, and one injury involving my elbows that I don't think anybody has even bothered to dream up a name for.

From my wife's point of view, every one of my wounds has been self-inflicted. I've had a lot of trouble getting her to understand how things really are, so I'll explain it to you. Then, if you'll be so kind, you can explain it to her.

It's just that all my life I've been the kind of meathead who is willing to lay down in front of a hard slap shot and take it in the ribs to prevent a goal in a pick-up hockey game. When nobody's keeping score. You should understand that I've never been a goalie – goalies are actually a different species, who are apparently genetically pre-disposed to do goofy things like that.

You might think that I exhibit a certain lack

of perspective when it comes to participating in sports. You would be right.

And I think my problem got a whole lot worse the day that I realized, at about the age of forty, that the odds had become pretty slim that the Detroit Tigers would be calling me to pitch short relief - especially since I haven't thrown a baseball since the late '60s.

To compensate, I began to charge headlong into every activity that even resembles a sport, throwing my body into the fray with the reckless abandon of a gladiator auditioning for a starting position in the Pompeii Lions lunch buffet.

Along the way I've also developed a fairly high tolerance for pain. This comes in pretty handy whenever I come up with a great idea for a new trick I want to try on shoe skis and all the drugstores are closed.

Now I'll bet there are lots of other kamikaze athletes like me out there. Well guys, I'm going to share with you the secret mantra I always use when I come to the sudden realization that the mountain bike trail I'm on is rated, "Are You Out Of Your Cotton-Picking Mind?" I simply close my eyes, transport myself to my "happy place," and say:

"Uh-oh. This is really gonna hurt..."

BONEHEDs Unite

A few weeks ago I suggested in this column that we should completely update the English Language. I mean, here we are text-messaging ourselves into the twenty-first century and we have to waste our time fooling around with outmoded concepts like "spelling," "grammar," and "punctuation."

My idea was to form a group called the Bureau Of Nearly Everybody Hacking English Down, or BONEHED.

Well, as you might suppose, I got a lot of feedback on that one. Here's one example:

Deer Mistur Funny Guy,

As Leedur of the Free World, you see, I unnerstand that I oughta rip yur arm off and beat u with the bloody stump.

Ha, ha, ha.

Seeriusly, I unnerstand what u mean about them Spel Chekrs. They nevur wurk rite. That's y I've appointed a krak team of guys who wurked on my my kampain to chek stuff like this note ovur for me. My dad was the eddukashun president, so I unnerstand the importens of gud gramur and spling.

Sinseerly, yur friend,

Name Withheld By Request,

The White House, Washington, DC.

I even got a call from my eighth-grade English teacher, Miss Knucklebuster. "Well, young man, I suppose you think you're smart," she said.

"Wow, Miss Knucklebuster," I replied. "I haven't seen you for more than forty years. And you weren't exactly a spring chicken back then! How come you're alive?"

"Well, I might as well not be, if you and all your little friends are going to go and ruin the English language. You always were kind of a meathead."

"That's BONEHED. And we're not ruining the language, just fixing it."

"Fixing it? I never considered it broken. Except for a little bit of word-rot I've noticed in the last few years."

"What do you mean?"

"Strange words keep popping up. Like 'Blog;' what the dickens does that mean?"

"It's short for 'Web Log.' It means that people who can't get their ideas published anywhere can put them on the Web. Then other people can read the blog and add their own un-publishable ideas."

"And that's a good thing?"

"Of course it is. It's information."

"Accurate information?"

"Well no, not necessarily. Bloggers can write pretty much whatever they feel like writing."

"And people who find factual errors can post their corrections?"

"Well they could, but the blogger would probably just delete them."

"So how do you know if a blogger is telling the truth?"

"If you agree with what he's saying, you assume it must be true."

"And if you don't agree?"

"You just start your own blog, and you write about what total jerks all the other bloggers are."

"And in all this blogging you can also ignore spelling and grammar?"

"That's the beauty of it! Lots of bloggers are BONEHEDs!"

Part I: Bikes, Docks & Slush Nuggets

"Indeed!"

"Anything else you'd like to know?" I was enjoying educating my former teacher.

"Bear with me," she said, "I wrote down another word with which I was unfamiliar. I have it here somewhere." I could hear Miss Knucklebuster digging around in her purse. "There, I found it. Oh yes. What is a 'podcast?'"

"It's the latest thing! Instead of taking all the time and effort to write things down for your blog, you just record an hour or so of yourself and maybe some friends mumbling things you believe to be clever, then you post the recording to the internet so people can download it and listen to it on their iPods."

"And why would they want to do that?"

"Usually because they hope that you will say something dirty."

There was a long pause on the other end of the line. Finally I said, "Miss Knucklebuster, are you all right?"

"Yes," she replied. "I was just sitting here listening to William Shakespeare spinning in his grave."

After she hung up I realized that I forgot to invite her to join BONEHED.

Butterfly

Last Friday I held a monarch butterfly on my finger and carried him out into the blinding afternoon sun.

I had first known him as a scrawny little caterpillar, crawling around on green leaves like an eating machine, converting what seemed like acres of milkweed into a big, juicy caterpillar. I watched him climb up and hang in the air for a whole day, looking as nervous as a caterpillar can look, working up the nerve to do what he had to do.

I watched that caterpillar turn himself inside out – I don't know any other way to describe it – and transform himself into that distinctive bright green monarch chrysalis, with the row of tiny gold nuggets across the side. And earlier last Friday I watched him fight his way out of his chrysalis, turned whisper-thin and transparent after hanging motionless for two weeks, then I watched him unfurl his monarch's gold and black wings.

I just got off the phone with my son. He was telling me that he was getting ready for his first real "I've-gotta-buy-a-suit-for-it" job interview. He wanted to know if he needed to wear a belt with the suspenders that came with that new suit. I told him not to, unless it was a gun belt.

As I hung up, I couldn't help thinking about the first time I held my son, minutes old and not much bigger than my two hands. I looked at his wizened little newborn-reptile face, and he looked at me with an expression that was every bit as amazed as I felt. I think we were sizing each other up. As luck would have it, we decided to go ahead and give it a shot.

I couldn't help thinking about watching that scrawny little infant crawling around the house like an eating machine, converting what seemed like acres of Cheerios and strained peas into a big, juicy kid.

I couldn't help thinking about standing him up on his Big Bike for the first time, or about taking him to get braces on his teeth. Or about buying us both rollerblades so I could teach him how to skate, then accidentally tripping him with my hockey stick so those brand new braces completely mangled the inside of his lips. Or about the day he informed me that I could no longer hug him in front of all the other kids when I dropped him off at school.

I couldn't help thinking about when he hit sixteen, and I watched him turn himself inside out – I don't know any other way to describe it – to transform himself into that distinctive moody, non-communicative teen-ager.

For the next few years I didn't really see too much of him. He always seemed to be "hanging out" with buddies, and didn't really have much to say.

And now he's bought himself a suit for a job interview. Even though he told me that it was light gray – with suspenders – I can't help picturing the jacket as somehow being monarch gold and black.

Last Friday when I held that butterfly up to the sun, I had to shake my finger a little bit to get him to let go. But when he did, he flexed those beautiful wings and soared away into the sky.

Part I: Bikes, Docks & Slush Nuggets

Caramel Apples, Yellow Jackets And Other Signs That Summer Is Over

October in Michigan is a magical thing. The leaves are beginning to change, the nights are cooler, and the kids are back in school. From the football stadium, the festive sounds of the marching band, the referee's whistle, the tearing of ligaments, and the snapping of bones fill the crisp autumn air.

We've all been spoiled by a long wonderful summer of warm-weather activities, when we could go out to the lake or the golf course or the chain gang on just about any afternoon and enjoy soaking up enough ultraviolet radiation to toast a bagel. But now the boats are snuggled away in their shrink wrap and the old nine iron is resting peacefully on the bottom of that pond near the green on number twelve. It's time to switch over to Fall Fun.

One thing I always like to do is visit the neighborhood Cider Mill And Yellow Jacket Wasp Preserve. This is a place where you can enjoy cinnamon donuts, caramel apples, fresh apple cider, and stinging insects motivated enough to swipe a Coney dog right off your paper plate.

I once knew a guy who became a legend by surviving three trips to the Cider Mill trash barrel in one afternoon! Unfortunately, on the fourth trip he had a couple of French fries stuck to the seat of his jeans – he disappeared into the cloud of wasps and was never seen again.

In the meantime, the hunters are all getting warmed up for deer season, blowing practice holes in Stop signs throughout the Midwest. As Opening Day draws nearer their workouts will get more intense, until they're blasting Yield signs and, eventually, the smaller and more elusive Speed Limit signs.

The deer are out in the woods doing wind sprints and other cardio, obviously working on building endurance and foot speed.

As I'm sure you know, the bow hunters always get the first crack at the deer. My friend Clyde "Drinks Much Budweiser" Thumpwell claims to be part Native American, and prefers hunting with a bow. He says, "It gives the deer a sporting chance."

When Clyde hunts he hides in a blind halfway up a tree wearing head-to-foot camouflage. He douses himself with doe urine to mask his scent. He uses a compound bow, equipped with a GPS-enabled laser targeting system. His bow is capable of pounding an arrow through the door of a Volkswagen. He fires scientifically designed arrows with the stopping power of a Patriot missile.

The only way the deer are going to get any chance, sporting or otherwise, is if Clyde Drinks a little too Much Budweiser and falls out of the tree.

Of course, you should never forget the lesser-known Autumn activities that are available to us. These include; Half-heartedly Congratulating People Whose Favorite Baseball Teams Made The Playoffs (a tradition in the Detroit area for many years); Jumping Into The Leaf Pile When The Neighbors Aren't Looking (only really fun if you avoid building the leaf pile on top of the lawn mower); and Reminding Yourself That You Only Have To Cut The Grass A Few More Times (if you could only find that darned lawn mower...).

So be creative. However you choose to occupy these golden days of Fall, just remember that the glories of Winter are just around the corner.

Aaaaaaaaarrrgggghhhhhh!

Dock Tales - The Fall

It's October, so a lot of people around here have already taken their stuff out of the water and stored it away for the winter. They did this on decent Autumn days when it was fairly pleasant to be in the lake. These are the same people who always wait to put their boats in until late Spring when the weather is warm enough that there was at least a remote chance someone would want to use them.

Weird, huh?

My friend Tom and I have a slightly different philosophy. We like to think of ourselves as pioneers, braving the extremes at both ends of the season as our own modest way of pushing back the Boundaries of Human Endeavor.

Not procrastination – Boundaries of Human Endeavor. Honest.

Part I: Bikes, Docks & Slush Nuggets

As a side note, does it seem fair to you that our friends who live in Florida never have to take their docks in and out? This is because the lakes don't freeze in Florida. At any time of the year, all they have to do to enjoy the water is go out and shoo the alligators and water snakes off the jet ski hoist.

Lucky devils.

Anyway, last spring when Tom and I put the dock in, we left a few small details that we knew were not quite perfect. There were a couple of cracked boards. A few of the poles were a little bent. The last fifty feet or so looked like we lined them up by tossing the poles and dock sections out of a helicopter. About twenty feet were under water.

"Relax," we told each other, basking in the optimistic sunshine of the springtime afternoon, "we've got all summer to tidy it up."

Well, sometime in June the cracked boards began to give way completely, so walking out to the boat became a little like playing a game of hopscotch in a minefield. In July the bent poles slipped, so from that point on you pretty much had to use climbing gear and safety ropes to traverse those spots. By about mid-August we'd come to think of the process of reeling along down the zigzags toward the end of the dock as a sort of personal folk dance.

Around the beginning of September our rationalization had subtly shifted from "We've got all summer..." to "Well, the season's almost over..."

And so, on a beautiful Saturday afternoon a few weekends ago we were standing on the dock, clinging to a pole to keep from sliding off, and Tom said, "You know, we really ought to think about taking the dock out."

"Yes," I replied, "we certainly should."

"So, you want to go skiing?"

"Sure."

As the autumn days rolled by we would spend more and more time each weekend carefully gauging the weather, monitoring the changing water temperature, calculating the lengths of the days, and discussing taking the dock out. Then we would decide to go and do something else.

And now we've started the job. So far we've spent one weekend dragging the hoists up on shore, then gesturing with our beer bottles at where we want to stack everything else. Next weekend the dock itself comes out.

You know, I think it's that above-mentioned Boundaries-Of-Human-Endeavor thing that compels us, after waiting until the water is really, really cold, to tackle the job in leaky waders.

These are the same waders, coincidentally, that we intended to replace after freezing in them last spring.

After all, we had all summer...

A Giant

I had a friend named Scott. He was a Giant.

He was one of the largest men I've ever known, with a body that could fill up a room or block out the sun. He once played Harry Potter's Giant, Hagrid, to my Professor Dumbledore, standing a good-natured, grumbling guard over stacks of new Harry Potter books, while wide-eyed young fans trembled in his shadow then asked kind old Dumbledore to sign autographs.

But his size wasn't what made him a Giant.

As you might expect of any good Giant, Scott wore a fierce, bristly beard that covered most of his face. The look could be so intimidating that you might not notice the eyes that twinkled through his wire-rimmed glasses. I believe he could actually make his beard flare on command, especially when he saw something that displeased him.

Part I: Bikes, Docks & Slush Nuggets

But that big fierce beard wasn't what made him a Giant.

He was a self-appointed peace maker. He could clear up just about any problem simply by striding into the middle of it. If he ever spotted someone who might be taking advantage of a weaker person, for any reason, he became an avenging Giant, and that would pretty much be the end of any advantage-taking.

But his ability to dominate a situation wasn't what made him a Giant.

What made Scott a Giant was just Scott. He was a private sort of Giant, so like many of his friends I was only privileged to see and share tiny bits of his life. He was a warrior in Vietnam. He was a policeman. Then he was a Giant working in a book store. And through all these incarnations, he was a husband and a father and a friend.

Like a Giant should be, he was proud, but his pride was rarely self-directed. He wasn't prone to talking all that much, and then rarely about himself without a lot of prodding. But he never got tired of telling his friends about the two people who occupied the center of his universe, his wife and his son. He was never happier than when he was delivering a dribble-and-shot account of young Scottie's basketball games.

What I've Learned So Far...

It's a personal source of pride to me that he loved my columns. Whenever he read a goofy one, his laughter would rumble like far-off thunder. Whenever he read one that tugged at his heart, he would come and find me, with tears streaming down his Giant face and disappearing into that fierce beard, and he'd say, "Ok, you got me!"

On those occasions it always surprised me that he was willing to share with the world the sight of a weeping Giant.

When I started writing this I had just been told that the decision had been made to take Scott off life support. I knew that it was his decision, and the right one, and I knew the probable outcome. But, like the dreamer that I am, I was hoping for some kind of miracle.

And when the word came that Scott had left this world, I felt sad, and diminished, and more than a little bit angry. I felt like I'd been cheated of my miracle, because I would never see my friend the Giant again.

But I was wrong. As I sit here and let my mind carry me back to the rumbling laughter and those tear-streaked cheeks, I realize that I got that miracle all right, and I'll bet everybody else who knew him can say the same. You see, we all experienced an amazing thing.

A Giant passed our way.

Part I: Bikes, Docks & Slush Nuggets

Halloween

I miss Halloween.

Ok, we still have the fun of handing out bags of goodies to the kids at the door, of filling every square foot of the yard with inflatable witches and goblins, and of going to Halloween parties where we all seem to believe that our friends won't recognize us in our Hugh Hefner and the Sexy Playmate costumes.

But it's just not like the old days.

First, I should explain that I have very fond memories of Halloweens when I was a child. This was many years ago, back when you could ring a neighbor's doorbell and yell, "Trick or treat!" without first having your buddies set up a diversion to draw fire, then lobbing a percussion grenade through a window.

Back then, my brother and I would each bring

home bags jammed with enough candy to keep an average school bus-load of kids buzzed on a serious carbohydrate high for a month. Like two little refined-sugar misers, we'd sit on the floor and sort our booty into carefully segregated heaps ranging from the Snickers and Almond Joys in the "keep-your-grubby-little-meat-hooks-off" pile, to the "let-the-dog-have-it" stack made up of "candy corn," baggies of stale popcorn, and those red-and-white round mint things like they have next to the register at the Chinese restaurant.

Then my dad would come by like a mafia don and collect his percentage. He was usually kind enough to bypass our top-echelon inventory and raid the mid-range stuff, concentrating his take somewhere around the level of Good 'N Plenty, Heath Bars, and black licorice whips. We didn't mind; we figured that since he had paid for the costumes, he was entitled to a taste of the action.

Then I began to grow up, and by the time I was twenty, the tried-and true people in charge of handing out the goodies stopped buying the "tall kid in a Casper The Friendly Ghost Mask" routine. I realized then that I was going to be pretty much out of luck until I had a kid of my own to do the bag work.

True, I could always dip into the bags of candy I bought to give away, but that just does not encompass the same spirit of adventure. Or the variety – how many inch-long Baby Ruth bars can one guy eat?

Now considering how well my dad did shaking down my brother and me, I decided that once I got married I would simply father twelve to fifteen kids, who could then be strategically deployed in handout-rich neighborhoods, like miniature commandos in Dracula suits.

Ok, so I didn't think to run the plan past my wife before we got married, just to make sure we were on the same page on that particular concept. As it turns out, we were not.

So instead of propagating our own little trick-or-treating platoon, we had one son. And while he was a valiant little vampire, even during his prime candy gathering years there was only so much loot even a highly motivated kid could bring into the organization on his own.

And now my son is grown and living away from home, presumably facing the same Halloween candy predicament as his old man. I guess we'll both just have to wait until he gets married and has kids.

So what's a grandpa's cut amount to, anyway?

Angel at a U2 Concert

She was probably a little too large to be a prom queen.

And her hair was probably a little too black, nothing like the beauty parlor blonde of prom queens. She had obviously had that too-black hair carefully cut and styled for the concert, but it was a short, sensible cut, not at all what a prom queen would require for a night at the Palace.

Her outfit was what you might call an "enthusiastic" shade of green. It was a color that the average prom queen would probably avoid in favor of pinks or whites or pastels. She was at the U2 concert with a couple of girl friends, who were also probably a little too large to be prom queens.

And she was gorgeous.

She stood in the front row of the pit, as close

as she could possibly get to where the stocky genius Rock Star marched up and down the stage in his bad haircut, purple shades, black jeans, sensible shoes, and leather jacket. She sang every word of every one of his brilliant songs in perfect synchronization with him, sometimes watching with a look that said that she could not believe what she was seeing, and other times closing her eyes and soaring into his lyrics, shaking her head from side to side with the music.

Every now and then the whole experience would seem to overwhelm her, and she would clutch the sides of her head as if she needed to hold it to keep it from exploding to the beat.

But she never stopped singing.

It would be easy to dismiss her as nothing more than a girl with a crush on a Rock Star. But I have to believe that the story behind her angelic face is a lot better than simple hero-worship.

You see, in the thunderous symphony of sounds and spotlights spilling from the stage, her face glowed with an even greater brilliance than the show we'd all paid to see. It was a glow generated deep in the heart of a young girl who was completely and perfectly happy – completely and perfectly involved – with where she was at that moment.

Not far from where I was standing, another girl about the same age as the black-haired angel in the pit brushed imagined lint off of her size-2 skirt. She tossed her perfect blonde hair and smiled indulgently at the activity on the stage and at her date. She had almost certainly been a prom queen. She bobbed her head with the beat, she held her cell phone up and waved it in time with the music when everyone else did, and she even tried valiantly to lip-sync part of one of U2's most popular songs. I'm sure she enjoyed the show.

But she didn't live the show.

You know, I can't help thinking about that angel in the pit with the too-black hair. I wonder if later, as the echoes of Bono's voice and the ringing in her ears faded away, as all the prom queens of the world reestablished their beautifully manicured domination over reality, if she had some way to recreate the pure joy that wrapped around her as she danced at the edge of that stage.

And I wonder if she's ever looked in a mirror and recognized in herself the radiant and pure beauty that she unselfishly beamed in the direction of the Rock Star – and the rest of us – on that night.

I hope so.

Bring Me Back A Bambi Burger

A few weeks ago in this column I mentioned bow hunting for deer. I pointed out that the concept of the bow hunter as a kind of modern-day Hiawatha, gliding through the forest and slaying the noble beast with a hand-hewn weapon, is not quite accurate when Hiawatha's hand-hewn weapon is equipped with a laser targeting system.

And now we're approaching the highlight of the year for all the really serious Bambi Blasters out there – the firearm deer season's Opening Day! Think of it! A million and-a-half guys in orange hats, a million and-a-half loaded weapons, and three million cases of beer – what could possibly go wrong?

Now please don't think that I'm making fun of hunters. I make it a point never to make fun of people who have guns and who like to shoot things with them.

Besides, there's nothing I enjoy more than tossing a nice venison steak on the grill, so I certainly can't claim any philosophical or moral objection to hunting. I'm just way too much of a wimp to do it. When I want a hamburger, I'd rather not have to club the cow and grind it up myself.

So while I don't hunt, I have nothing but respect for the average hunter. Here is an outdoorsman who can survive for a week or more on nothing but Twinkies, Slim Jims, and Bud Light. He can sleep in a drafty cabin filled with seven other snoring guys and a cloud of Slim Jim farts. He can get up before dawn, sit shivering in the woods all day without ever seeing a deer, then happily go back to camp for another night of snoring and flatulence.

And he looks forward to this all year.

Just this morning I ran into my hunter friend, Thor. "So," I said, "do you have all your guns and ammo ready for Opening Day?"

"Nah," Thor said, looking like he'd just lost his best Winchester. "I'm not going hunting this year."

"Really? Why not?"

"Aw, my son's getting married next weekend. In Maui. Darned kid."

"That sounds expensive."

"Not really. The bride's parents are paying for the plane tickets, the room..."

"The whole shot?"

Thor looked pained. "Don't say 'shot!'"

"Sorry."

"Anyway, we gotta fly out to Maui on Opening Day! And we have to be out there for two whole weeks!"

"Don't you like the girl?"

"No, she's great. In fact, we kind of wonder what she sees in our son."

"Wow, a week in Maui, all expenses paid, to see your son get married to a terrific girl. How inconsiderate can these people get?"

"I know it. Hey, do you suppose there might be any deer camps near Lahaina?"

"Maybe you should pack a rifle or two. You know, just in case."

Of course, Opening Day also means that there will be some nimrod out there who will get all tanked up and take a potshot at a Durango or somebody's Schnauzer. But cheer up - it seems like sooner or later the basic principles of natural selection always weed guys like that out of the gene pool.

So for all you hunters who are trembling with anticipation, polishing your hollow-points and stocking up on Slim Jims, I have just five words:

Have fun, and be safe.

Here We Are – The Pilgrims' Pride

The car pulls into Great Aunt Ellen's driveway at exactly five minutes after eleven on a fine Thanksgiving morning. Since the moment the family left the house, an hour before dawn this morning, Todd Junior and Little Suzie have been passing the hours playing festive travel games, alternating between the traditional "Let's Make Little Suzie Cry!" and the ever popular "Mom, Todd's Making Me Cry!"

Before the car has quite rolled to a stop, Mom, Todd Junior and Little Suzie are out and sprinting for the bathroom. Dad, who apparently has a much larger bladder, joins Great Uncle Charlie and Uncle Fred in the garage where they are squatting on the floor and studying the directions for a brand-new turkey fryer.

What I've Learned So Far...

Great Aunt Ellen has arranged fifteen fire extinguishers at strategic points around the garage. Now she's standing behind the men, explaining how a story she saw on the six o'clock news proved that frying a turkey in the garage is twice as dangerous as tossing a burning road flare into a bathtub full of napalm.

Grandpa is sitting in a recliner in the living room watching the Macy's Thanksgiving Day Parade on TV. Grandpa is wearing a flannel shirt, wool pants, two pairs of socks, insulated work boots, and long johns. Grandpa has adjusted the thermostat so that the air in the living room is hot enough to curl the wallpaper.

Grandma, Mom, Aunt Karen and Aunt Meg are in the kitchen making things like pumpkin pies and mashed potatoes. Aunt Meg had wanted to make a mincemeat pie, but Grandma reminded her that Uncle Stan is bringing his new girlfriend, and she's some kind of a vegetarian, and insisted that they stick with pumpkin.

Before long Todd Junior has drafted Karen's boy Sheldon and Aunt Meg's twins into a rousing game of "Let's Catch Little Suzie And Tickle Her 'Till She Pees!" In her seven years on Earth as Todd Junior's little sister, Little Suzie has developed the survival skills of a ninja, so she locks all four boys in the basement and settles

Part I: Bikes, Docks & Slush Nuggets

down to play Barbies with her cousins Brittany and Pammie.

The men carefully lower the turkey into the hot oil as Great Aunt Ellen falls to her knees and pleads for salvation. Aunt Meg tries without success to convince Grandma that mincemeat is not really meat, and besides they're having turkey, which is really meat, so she doesn't see the problem. Aunt Karen becomes a little hysterical when she realizes that you don't get gravy when you deep-fry the turkey, but Mom and Aunt Meg calm her down by opening another bottle of White Zinfandel.

Carl the Dog, lying on the floor next to Grandpa's chair, suffers a heat stroke.

And then, at last, the feast is ready. Uncle Stan and his girlfriend Stacey show up just as Great Uncle Charlie brushes the last of the white fire extinguisher stuff off the turkey and fires up the electric carving knife. After a fairly intensive cross-examination by Aunt Meg, it turns out that Stacey's a veterinarian, not a vegetarian, and mincemeat pie would have been just fine with her — maybe even her absolute favorite.

As soon as Thanksgiving Dinner is over, Uncle Stan and Stacey excuse themselves to go celebrate Thanksgiving with Stacey's relatives. Grandma won't let them go to their second turkey dinner of the afternoon without sending along a huge ziploc bag full of leftovers.

The women all hug and kiss Stacey goodbye, then they go to the kitchen to clean up the dishes and discuss what a selfish skank Stacey is to drag Stan away from his family on Thanksgiving.

The men join Grandpa in the living room, where the paint on the ceiling is beginning to blister, and sprawl about in nests of couch pillows and perspiration to snore through a couple of football games.

Little Suzie traps Todd Junior and the other boys in an upstairs linen closet, then joins the girls to resume the Barbies marathon.

And all is right with the world.

Part I: Bikes, Docks & Slush Nuggets

A Dictionary for BONEHEDs

Not too long ago on this page we formed a group called the Bureau Of Nearly Everybody Hacking English Down. Since then prospective BONEHEDs have contacted me from every part of the country, enlisting in the noble effort to escort our version of the English language – in shackles, kicking and screaming if necessary – into the twenty-first century.

Last week I got a text message about BONEHED on my cell phone. This was my first text message ever (other than the one that came with the phone, which welcomed me to the incredible world of text messaging, and which is still on my phone because I don't have any idea how to delete it).

The message, from a young woman, read:

What I've Learned So Far...

DEER MR FNYGY

Y I OTTA RYAOABYWTBS. U GOT TH ABRVS RONG. U R A WOMBAT

H&K, YR FAN, JESSICA

Ok, I'll admit this one had me completely baffled, until I got my son to help me translate it:

DEER MR FNYGY = Dear Mr. Funny Guy

Y I OTTA = Why I ought to

RYAOABYWTBS = rip your arm off and beat you with the bloody stump

U GOT TH ABRVS RONG = You got the abbreviations wrong

U R A = You are a

WOMBAT = You know, it's a funny thing; by the time we got to this one I thought I was getting the hang of this whole deal, so I figured that this meant Wonderful, Outstanding Man, Brilliant And Talented. Not quite. It means Waste Of Money, Brains And Time.

H&K = Hugs and kisses

YR FAN = Your Fan

JESSICA = Mary

Well Mary, I'm glad to have you for a fan, and I welcome you to BONEHED. All I have to say is, "My HIHIS" (My Head Is Hanging In Shame) – next time I'll try to get the abrvs ryt.

Part I: Bikes, Docks & Slush Nuggets

This whole incident has me wondering if there are occasions when sending a text message may not be such a great idea. Like this:

JOHN

I M DMPNG U.

MARCIA

Here Marcia appears to be breaking off some sort of romantic relationship with John. This is her prerogative, of course, but doing it this way seems a bit harsh and impersonal. It would be much kinder for her to communicate this message, with its many underlying emotional implications, in lipstick on the bathroom mirror.

Here's another example:

DEER KIM,

U R 4 ME. WIL U B MY M8?

WELL, IGTR (I've Got To Run), *BILL*

Here Bill is clearly proposing marriage to Kim, but it seems like there must be a more romantic way to go about it. For instance, he could find a cool picture of a penguin wearing a top hat holding an engagement ring, then email it to her.

Other questionable uses for text messaging might include a Summons:

U R ORDRD 2 APEER

... a thank-you note:

DEER ANT RUTH,

THNX,

BOBBIE

... bad news:

U R GONNA CROAK

... good news:

OOPS, I MENT 2 DIAL YR B-I-L (brother-in-law) *4 THAT CROAK THNG*

... or suicide notes:

C YA

In any case, it is clear that we need to set some standards for our proud new version of the English language – and we BONEHEDs are just the folks to do it! If all of you readers would email me with your favorite acronyms and abbreviations, I'll put them together for us into a BONEHED's dictionary. Send your ideas to bonehed@learnedsofar.com.

Merriam-Webster, eat your heart out!

Part I: Bikes, Docks & Slush Nuggets

Holiday Horrors: Visa Bills, Fruitcakes, And Those Mind-Numbing Family Newsletters

You feel the familiar dread coming over you as you pull it out of the envelope - eight sheets of pink paper, covered on both sides with microscopic gray type. These pages chronicle the past twelve months in the lives of your Aunt Edith and Uncle Jake, covering everything they've done that was more significant than eating breakfast (and they've gone ahead and documented what they consider their more memorable breakfasts).

It's the Holiday Newsletter.

Reading it, you will discover that Edith and Jake's oldest boy, Carl, is planning to go to either community college or medical school, as soon as he finishes up his GED and his ninety days of community service. You learn all about the egg-candling class Aunt Edith took with her friend Sylvia, and about Uncle Jake bowling a lifetime-high 130 game in the Wednesday Night Elks Club Bowling League.

All of your questions are answered regarding George the Gerbil's cute little quadrupal coronary bypass surgery.

So how can you defend yourself against this eye-crossing hemorrhage of family information? One obvious idea would be to simply discard it unread. The problem with this is that there are always little diligence bombs planted on every page, and Aunt Edith is an expert interrogator;

"So, did you get the Newsletter?"

"Sure did, Aunt Edith. It was... um... great."

"And?"

"And what, Aunt Edith?"

"You know. Applesauce."

"Oh, of course. Applesauce. It's... um, great?"

"Your cousin Ralph gets run over and crippled by a truckload of applesauce and you think it's 'great'?"

And just like that, you're out of the will.

My suggestion is to try aversion therapy. Just send all the newsletter-writers in your circle of friends and family a taste of their own medicine.

Part I: Bikes, Docks & Slush Nuggets

Here are a few general Newsletter Themes you might use:

The "Tobacco Road" – see how much misfortune you can pack into a #10 envelope; "...We weren't too upset when the garage burned down, since the car was already repossessed and all. After that, things got a mite better for a few days, until the following Tuesday, when Jethro had one of his spells and the septic tank blew up..."

The "General Hospital" – the more intimate medical details you can provide, the better; "...and then I figure, what the heck, since we're at the doctor's to have him look at Emma's piles anyway, let's just go ahead and get that boil on my own butt lanced..."

The "Pet Parade" – no incident is insignificant when it comes to the little darlings; "...hairballs don't really bother me that much, but Ed gets real upset when the cat hocks one into his dress shoes, so we decided to have little Muffikins shaved..."

The *"Travelogue"* – paint them a vivid picture of the places you've been; "...You might not think that Toxic Waste, Oklahoma would be that great of a vacation spot, but we find that it's just about the most romantic thing you can imagine to sit in lawn chairs next to the camper, just after sunset, gazing off to the West at the warm, green glow coming off the landfill..."

The "Incomprehensible" – keep them guessing; "...so then I told them that four hundred dollars was way too much for a vasectomy on a weekday in March, and anyway, General Motors products are definitely more reliable than giving away lab rats at the Farmers' Market..."

Of course if all else fails, you can always just change your name, shave your head and move to Tibet. Just don't leave a forwarding address, and don't make friends with any monks who keep mailing lists.

Part I: Bikes, Docks & Slush Nuggets

Dodging The Christmas Shopping Bullet – The Five Deadliest Things You Could Buy Your Wife For Christmas

Ok, we're in it now. There's snow on the ground and every public building you walk into has Bing Crosby crooning about it. Holiday cards have started coming in from all those maniacs who are organized enough to get their holiday cards out before St. Patrick's Day. Everywhere you go there's someone walking around wearing a "Let's Kill 'Em All And Let God Sort 'Em Out" sweat shirt and a Santa hat. Visions of eggnog (with just a wee splash of rum) are dancing in my head.

Yep, it's Christmas season all right, and it's time to think about shopping.

What I've Learned So Far...

Ok, confession time. Just because I'm thinking – and writing – about Christmas shopping sixteen days before Christmas doesn't mean I'm doing any sort of actual shopping yet. I still have 15.75 days before that becomes a major issue, so I'm biding my time.

Now, my wife shops for me and for everyone else on our family gift list, while all I have to do is buy something for her. You would think that this would make the gifting thing a simple and straightforward task.

You would be wrong.

You see, to me Christmas shopping is a sacred ritual, steeped in almost holy tradition. That, and a good healthy sense of terror. I've been married long enough to know that buying a gift for your wife can represent one of the most treacherous transactions in a man's life.

Now, I'll admit that for the first year or two your little newlywed bride might think your stupidity is just adorable when she unwraps the hot pink left-handed salad shooter you bought from the guy in the mall kiosk, who told you that this was the one gift every woman lives for. But once the honeymoon's over, Buster, things change.

So for those of you guys for whom the grace period has expired, I've compiled this list of the five deadliest things you could give to your wife

Part I: Bikes, Docks & Slush Nuggets

for Christmas:

1. A Vacuum Cleaner – A gift like this suggests that you think of her as some kind of unpaid servant, which is normally a really bad thing for you to let her know. This warning would also apply to mops, brooms, monogrammed scrub brushes, and plow yokes with shackles on them.

2. A Diet Book Or A Gift Certificate To Weight Watchers – Likewise, you should avoid self-help books with titles like, I'm Ok, But You're Getting Pretty Hefty or 30 Days To A Slimmer, Less Disgusting You. Do I really have to explain why?

3. Slutty Underwear – This is a particularly bad idea if the slutty underwear is not her size. Buy it too large, and you'll be in the same mess as you were in with the diet book, etc. Buy it too small, and she might think you got the boxes mixed up and get real curious about who you meant it for. If you're slick you can actually turn this one around, though, because you can always fall back on the old, "You see Honey, the beautiful, shapely young clerk asked me 'What size?' and I said, 'Well, she looks just like you...'"

4. Enhancement Surgery – You know exactly what I'm talking about. The people who sell enhancement surgery call it (this is true) "The Gift That Keeps On Giving." The question she'll have

for you is, "Yeah, well who exactly will it keep on giving to?"

5. A Tattoo — Particularly if you're thinking of sedating her with Tequila and having a scantily clad lady with the words "Live Hard, Die Young" tattooed on her forearm while she's unconscious.

So there you have it, guys. Now that I've clued you in on what not to buy, you can go out and get your wife anything else that strikes your fancy with complete confidence. For my wife, I'm thinking about two tickets to the North American Beer Chugging And Choral Belching Semi-Finals next month in North Dakota.

Don't tell her!

Dear Readers:

As we approach the new year, pretty much everybody with a word processor is doing a Year In Review column. They're trying to make us relive a bunch of stuff we're just glad to have made it through the first time. Not me! To commemorate the new year I've decided to grab my crystal ball, along with that bottle of Irish whiskey I got for Christmas, and take you on a voyage into the future. Welcome to:

2006 – The Year In Preview

January – Scientists at the National Institute of Health discover that radiation from the wildly popular Apple iPod causes users to turn into silhouettes that dance around hysterically (but well). While many officials are concerned about this phenomenon, iPod sales skyrocket as millions of women buy them for dancing-challenged white male husbands and boyfriends.

February – Tom DeLay finally completes his legal haggling and goes to trial before a judge, jury and court staff consisting entirely of Republican campaign workers. He decides that constant smirking and swaggering haven't done enough to demonstrate how confident he is, so on the first day of the trial he borrows Michael Jackson's SUV and moonwalks on the roof.

March – The Bird Flu has still not made its predicted deadly assault on mankind. However, the Center For Disease Control announces that cases of Bird Sniffles have appeared in Patterson, New Jersey, when a parakeet and two Cockatoos develop runny beaks.

April – Motorola unveils the "Razor II" cell phone, billed as "... The thinnest, sharpest wireless device ever." The new phone is quickly recalled when hundreds of people using them in cars hit potholes and slice off their ears.

May – The Republican campaign workers convict Tom DeLay on all counts with which he is charged. He immediately seeks an appeal based on the fact that it is rumored that the bailiff's great uncle might have voted for Truman.

June – The must-have Father's Day gift of

2006 is the Microsoft Digital Lawn Mower. The device is cool-looking, shiny and compact, but it has an unfortunate habit of freezing up just when you get to an interesting spot in the lawn.

July – In a July 4th speech George W. Bush vigorously attacks critics of the Iraq war, drawing parallels with America's struggle for independence and saying that car bombs are just "...those darn playful Iraqis' version of our Bottle Rocket."

August – Absolutely nothing happens, since everybody is on vacation.

September – Blackberry, the makers of the business-essential combination of a cell phone and a personal digital assistant, launches a new model aimed at "Executives on the Run," who may be too busy to stop for lunch. This revolutionary device, called the "Snackberry," dispenses reliable instant communications, along with an order of Bennigan's Pot Stickers.

October – Force-five hurricane "Marvin" lifts Mississippi, Alabama and Louisiana completely off the Gulf coast and drops them in western Ontario. Miraculously, nobody is injured, and they all decide to stay in Canada for the Molson and the free health care.

November – The Congressional midterm elections arrive, and for the first time in history every contest ends up in a tie. This activates a little-known clause in the Constitution which requires Ed Gillespie, chairman of the Republican National Committee and Howard Dean, chairman of the Democratic National Committee, to fight to the death during halftime of a Washington Redskins game. Ironically, when they fight everybody in the United States is out making a sandwich, and nobody cares enough afterward to find out what happened.

December – A story in the New York Times reveals that since 2002 the NSA has been monitoring domestic Christmas cards at the request of Bill O'Reilly, who asserts that the ones which say, "Happy Holidays" instead of "Merry Christmas" are "Ho-Ho-Helping The Yuletide Terrorists." Coincidentally, the CIA treats the entire editorial staff of the Times to an all-expenses-paid vacation at a secret "Holiday Resort" in Bulgaria.

So there you have it folks, everything you could ever need to know about the twelve months we have ahead of us. If I've overlooked anything, just try to deal with it.

Have a happy and safe New Year!

Part I: Bikes, Docks & Slush Nuggets

Stupid Winter Hats

You know, to me the worst thing about a Midwestern winter is not the gray skies. It's not the freezing rain, or the snow, or the sleet, or skidding on one heel across a parking lot clutching a bag of groceries in one arm and doing the "windmill prayer" (Oh God, oh God, oh God...) with the other.

It's the stupid winter hats.

Now, we are all aware of the double-blind scientific studies conducted by generations of Midwestern mothers which prove that at least 170% of your body heat escapes through your head. Apparently all that heat erupts right through your hair like a roman candle, and once it's all gone you "catch your death of cold."

According to this carefully-documented research, a hat serves as a sort of "body heat bottle cap." As a result, every Midwestern child grows up duty-bound to keep some kind of lid twisted onto his or her head from Thanksgiving through about a week before Easter.

As you have probably already noticed, most kids can get away with wearing clothing, especially hats, that make them look like little trolls or Oompa-Loompas. You can plop just about anything on their little melons and they end up being "cute." And the same is true for most women – remember how adorable Diane Keaton looked in Annie Hall?

As for me, looking "cute," or even halfway decent in a hat has never been a particularly realistic goal. If you were to put that same Annie Hall hat on me, within seconds you would have the neighbors dialing up the Help! There's a Psychotic Pervert On My Block hotline.

Here, in detail, are some of the headgear "looks" I've experimented with over the years:

The Elmer Fudd – If you're anywhere near as old as I am (hint – I now measure my age in "geological periods" rather than "years") your mom might have put you in one of these gems when you were about seven. This hat is kind of like a baseball cap with a flat top and ear flaps, and it makes a fashion statement that cries out, "Beat me up and take my lunch money."

Part I: Bikes, Docks & Slush Nuggets

The Toque – For those of you who have never spent time "Up North" or in Canada, a "toque" is one of those wool beanies like the one sported by that Waldo character everybody wants to find. Around here we call them "stocking caps." Some young guys, like my son, can yank one of these down to their eyebrows and look good, albeit a bit sinister. Not me. Even without the mask and the horizontal-striped shirt I wind up looking like a cartoon burglar.

The Cossack – Big furry hats might look terrific on gold miners, polar explorers and Russian Prime Ministers, but they make me look like I was involved in an unfortunate incident involving angular momentum and the hindquarters of a sheep dog.

The Great Detective – This is that tweed hat with the droopy brim and ear flaps worn by Sherlock Holmes. It is called a "Deerstalker," presumably because any deer catching sight of you with this thing on your head would be laughing so hard that it would make an easy target. I once tried a cousin of the deerstalker, introduced to the world by Inspector Jacques Clouseau in the Pink Panther movies. Every time I wore it I got attacked in my parlor by a little Chinese guy.

Besides these major millinery themes I've tried lots of other, less classic options, ranging from fluffy ear muffs (OK, they were pink) to cowboy hats. I've even tried combinations – it turns out, a pair of fluffy pink ear muffs worn with a cowboy hat also gets you beat up. On the up side, the guys who beat you up for this hardly ever take your lunch money.

So there you have it. Even though my mother's not around any more to supervise my cranial thermodynamics, I'm still trying to find something I could wear on my head to honor her memory without subjecting the lady next door to permanent psychological damage.

Any suggestions?

One Good Blog Deserves Another

When I was a kid, my parents loved to humiliate me by hugging me in public, or to crush my dreams of glory by keeping me from sky-diving off the tool shed with a bath towel parachute. Back then, the only way I had to get even with them was to wait until they weren't looking, then drink directly out of the milk carton. If I was really mad I would eat a cookie first – and backwash.

When I became a parent, I assumed that my son was working with the same set of options, so for eighteen years I just stayed away from the milk. And I've always figured that by the time the kid gets the chance to pick out which nursing home I'm going to end up in, his psychoanalyst will have taken some of the edge off the emotional trauma I inflicted by not buying him that dirt bike when he was in the third grade.

I never dreamed that I might get "blogged."

For those of you who are not yet familiar with blogging, this is an activity in which a person publishes a personal diary or "log" on the Web – a "Web log." If you repeat "web log" over and over with a mouth full of Tostitos, you get crap all over your keyboard.

You can write about that on your blog.

Blogging has opened up important new possibilities for the free interchange of critical information in our society. For instance, as I'm writing these words, the blog management Web site "Blogger.com" lists 3,589,074 posts about cats. Yes, without her blog, Lindsey Applegate of Cincinnati, Ohio would have no way of sharing with the rest of us those vital photographs of little Sammy, Cocoa, Cassie, Stinky, and Zoro (sic).

And there are many other topics diligently covered by bloggers throughout the world. Right now on Blogger.com there are:

674,050 posts about meat;

56,034 posts about toenails;

148,966 posts about stop signs;

17,344 posts about ear wax;

12,306 posts about scabs;

10,548 posts about boogers;

and 45 posts that discuss the pros and cons of both scabs and boogers!

As you can see, the informative potential of blogs is almost limitless.

So you can imagine my excitement when I discovered an entire blog created by my son, dedicated to me. A tribute, I thought, to the years I spent nurturing his growth, developing his character, and keeping the credit cards handy.

And then I discovered the title and overall theme of his blog; it's called "My Dad Is A Dork."

Now, I've been told that I was a dork on a regular basis for a sizeable chunk of my adult life. In fact, as my son grew up I actively developed my own signature brand of dorkiness, elevating embarrassing the kid to something of a fine art. I drove a Volvo, wore flip-flops to the grocery store, sold the Volvo and bought a PT Cruiser, and on one occasion – in perhaps the crowning triumph of my dorkosity – called my son "Sweetie" in a hockey locker room.

So I guess I can live with having my achievements in dorkdom celebrated and commemorated online. It's just a shame that he's away at college now. Otherwise I'd start another blog of my own and call it, "My Kid Is Soooooooo Grounded!"

*What I've Learned So Far...*

The Dorky Dad Factor

Last week in this column we tackled the use of "blogs" by "Generation Y," or "Generation Z" or "Generation Shrek" or whatever Generation it is that our kids belong to. I mentioned that they could use these blogs to get even with us for inflicting them with unspeakably cruel childhood torments, like crunchy peanut butter, skim milk, and whole wheat bread.

I also pointed out that my son is apparently a leader in this movement with his blog, tenderly titled "My Dad Is A Dork" (believe me, it could have been a whole lot worse).

Well, I got a little feedback on that column:

Dear Mr. Funny Guy,

Why, I ought to rip your arm off and beat you with the bloody stump.

Part I: Bikes, Docks & Slush Nuggets

Then I ought to use it to illustrate the true meaning of the word, "dork." According to wordorigins.org, popular etymology would have it that this American slang term comes from a word meaning a whale's penis. That is half right...

You no good commie.

Your Friend,

Leslie Merriam-Webster

Thanks for the information, Mr. Merriam-Webster. But if it's all the same to you, I'd just as soon not know the other half of that definition.

Anyway, every kid who ever lived understands the modern meaning of the word "dork," and we dads are proud to live up to the title. In fact, we actually belong to a secret society dedicated to the perpetual misery of our offspring.

Yes kids, when you were born, we all signed a contract, and agreed to adhere to a strict code of conduct. And now, at great risk to myself, I've decided to bend the rules on the Dorky Dad code of secrecy and share this document with you!

International Society of Fatherhood Dedicated Dorky Dad Document

What I've Learned So Far...

I, _____, parent of _____, do solemnly vow that I will humiliate my offspring every time I get the chance. I will achieve this goal by finding every way I can to be a certifiably uncool idiot, moron, doofus, fool, buffoon, clod, clown, and/or dork.

To accomplish this we will:

1. Dress in things your child would never wear. For example, an ensemble consisting of flip-flops, khaki Dockers, a purple Disney World T-Shirt and a green derby with "Kiss Me, I'm Irish" on it. This should guarantee deep and permanent emotional scarring.

2. Dress in things your child would be willing to wear. Sagging super-big pants (in my case, super super big) and a No Doubt T-shirt can be powerful trauma-inducing tools.

3. Don't dress at all. Yikes.

4. Use pet names or otherwise show affection for your offspring in public. The word "Sweetie" used to address a fifteen-year-old boy is a guarantee of at least a decade of psychiatric treatment in the years to come.

5. Drive a "nerdmobile." This would be any car other than the one your kid's best friend's dad, who also owns a condo in Maui, drives.

6. Make it your business to know every item

Part I: Bikes, Docks & Slush Nuggets

or brand name that kids think is desirable, then buy just the opposite. The ultimate insult would be to buy a teenager clothing or shoes from the dollar store with brand names like "Abercrummy" or "No Balance."

7. Greet your daughter's dates with lines like, "I collect guns and shovels. Guess which order I'll use them in if you bring my daughter home late?"

8. Attempt to learn about all the things that interest your kids, then being sure to get it just a little bit wrong. For example, if they are into extreme sports, tell all their friends that you really admire Tony Hawkeye.

9. Walk up to your child standing with a group of his or her friends and say something like, "What-up, Dawg?" Believe me, talking "street" will sound even dumber when you do it than it does when they do it.

I further attest and affirm that I will document any new developments in the field of fatherly dorkitude, and that I will share these developments with all other members of the International Society of Fatherhood.

Signed: _____

Date: _____

What I've Learned So Far...

Witnessed: _____

Date: _____

So there you have it, kids. The secret of your father's dorkiness is out. Just do me a favor and don't tell anybody where you heard about it.

Lord of the Five Rings

Hi. My name is Mike, and I'm an Olympaholic.

Now I'm aware that some of you might be a little bit indifferent to the Winter Olympics that are just winding down right now in Turin, Italy. According to the NBC ratings, that would be about 99.8% of you.

But I just can't help it. I'm hopelessly hooked on spending two weeks every four years fanatically watching people I've never heard of, doing things I won't even remotely care about again for the next two hundred and six weeks.

I'm not really sure why.

It might be because I know I'm watching people who are the best in the world at whatever it is they are doing. You pretty much have to respect a guy who is the best in the world at flopping onto a coaster sled and hurtling head-first down a chute of solid ice at more than eighty miles per hour. At the bottom of the hill, instead of psychological treatment this guy gets a gold medal.

I guess I have a soft spot in my heart for these athletes partly because I had the good fortune to make it to the "elite" level in the sport of pairs water skiing, The sport is a lot like pairs figure skating, but with less Russian mafia involvement.

Pairs water skiing is not an Olympic event, but my partners and I did get to compete in the very top tournaments, and we won our share of championships. Once, after skiing at Cypress Gardens and winning the Florida State tournament, a little girl even asked us for our autographs. It's kind of fun to think that the photo we signed for her that day might at this moment be lying quietly in a drawer, waiting to be discovered years from now by the woman grown from that little girl. She'll pick it up, look at it, smile wistfully, and say, "Geeze. Who the heck are these strange people?"

Anyway, I can actually relate when I watch ice skaters in spandex and sequins doing on the ice what my partners and I tried to do on the water – making hard, sweaty, dangerous tricks look smooth, easy, and beautiful.

But it is not just about the sport that is like my own. For the past two weeks I've been

Part I: Bikes, Docks & Slush Nuggets

grabbing every available moment to watch athletic spectacles like "Curling," where men or women wearing Dockers and golf shirts shove big round stones with handles on them down the ice and scream things like, "Yeeeeeeeeeeeeeeeeep," and "Huuuuuuuurrrrrrrryyyyy," while other men or women in Dockers and golf shirts scoot along down the ice with the stones and scrub like crazy with little brooms.

I've also been watching things like the "Biathlon," where people race through the woods on cross-country skis until they can barely stand up, stopping now and then to take a few shots at a target with a rifle. I guess this is practice for the Nordic equivalent of road rage.

Go ahead - insert your favorite "Buckshot" Cheney joke here...

I've been watching people hit a jump and throw themselves forty feet straight up into the air on skis, spinning and flipping around like a gum wrapper in a tornado, then losing points because they bent their knees a little bit too much when they crashed back to the snow. I've been watching long, muscular people in Spandex suits rocketing on skates around long, sleek tracks, and short, muscular people elbowing and crashing on skates around short, sleek tracks.

I've watched people sail off a huge ramp on

huge skis then turn their bodies into wings while they drop 20 stories to the snow, trying to fly a little further and make it to 20.00125 stories.

But I guess the Olympic athlete I admire the most is the one who is the thirty-fifth best in the world at diving down that chute of ice, or flipping around like a gum wrapper, or rocketing around the track, or dropping 20 stories. This is the person who never had any chance at all of landing a Nike commercial, yet goes out and puts it all on the line anyway.

Think about it. Most of the people who finish way back in the pack in these sports have spent a major part of their lives getting good enough at whatever they do to make it to the Olympics. They left gallons of sweat in the gym, they made all the necessary sacrifices, and they took all the necessary risks, knowing that they would probably never wind up riding down Main street, sitting on the back of a convertible and holding a medal up in the air and waving at a cheering crowd.

They've gone for years knowing that if they tell a stranger, "I'm a Luger," they are most likely to hear, "Um, I'm an Aquarius."

Now, after going to Italy and finishing 35th, they can say, "I'm an Olympian." Everybody should know what that means.

And The Camera Zoomed In – All The Way In

I recently had my first colonoscopy.

Ta-daa!

Ok, I admit we're not talking about coming home with a Pulitzer here, but I'm still pretty darned proud of myself.

For those of you who may be unfamiliar with the procedure, a colonoscopy involves doctors shoving a tiny (hopefully) television camera up the old pooter so they can have a look around. They are looking for early signs of colorectal cancer. This is a disease that, according to the American Cancer Society, kills 50,000 people in the United States each year - one every 9.3 minutes - although I'm not really sure how they get it paced out nice and even like that.

Apparently, if the doctors can find pre-cancerous polyps or catch the cancer in its early stages, colorectal cancer is pretty treatable, and your chances of survival are good. If they don't catch it early - well, one every 9.3 minutes...

And so a lot of doctors recommend that pretty much everyone over 50 should get a colonoscopy, especially if there is some family history of cancer.

Now on general principle, I've always felt that having things, especially television cameras, shoved up my old pooter was something to avoid at any cost, so I've been dodging colonoscopies for years - to the point where I was arguably risking my life. This year, I guess I finally just ran out of excuses.

The first thing that happened after I scheduled my colonoscopy was that a nice young woman called me. In a cheerful, even sexy, voice she introduced herself, then we spent about fifteen minutes chatting about my bowel movements. She was a good listener, and I found myself telling her things about my bowel movements that I've never shared with anyone before.

Finally, she gave me a little pep talk and told me that a packet of information I would need to review before the procedure would be coming in the mail. This made me a little nervous, because I never before had a medical test that I would have

Part I: Bikes, Docks & Slush Nuggets

to study for.

It turns out that the information packet gave me detailed instructions on how to flush myself completely clean before the procedure. I had to dine on only clear liquids the night before, then spend the next morning drinking a whole gallon of a special solution. This wasn't terrible, but I can tell you that it's not all that easy to drink a whole gallon of something you really like, much less something that tastes like thin lime kool-aid out of an old canteen.

Anyway, this gallon of stuff pretty much went through me like water through a fire hose, and it soon became apparent that I was really well rinsed out inside. This gave me a great sense of accomplishment, and left me walking a little bit bow-legged.

When we got to the clinic, they took me into a little room and had me change into one of those hospital gowns that is basically a great big bib with armholes. I stretched out on a really comfortable bed on wheels and relaxed while a pleasant nurse started an IV and commented on how nice I looked in a great big bib with armholes.

Before long they wheeled me into a bigger room with a lot of equipment and a large television monitor. Another pleasant nurse injected the anesthetic into my IV while she

What I've Learned So Far...

explained what was going to happen next. By the time all the anesthetic had been injected, I realized that I didn't really much care what was going to happen next, and that this nurse was actually beyond very pleasant - that she was in fact the nicest person I ever met.

Then the doctor came in, and it turns out *he* was the nicest person I ever met.

Everything after that is a little vague. I remember watching the exploration of a really cool-looking cave on the television monitor, and asking the nurse if it reminded her of the old movie Journey To The Center Of The Earth. I remember the doctor telling me that he had found a polyp, and watching him snip it off with a little lasso thingy, while I sang,

"Sixteen tons, and what do 'ya get?

"Another day older, and deeper in debt..."

And then after a while they were finished, and they wheeled me, possibly singing the Rum-Tum-Tugger song from Cats, out to a recovery room, where I explained to my wife that the doctor and nurse were the nicest people I ever met, even though neither of them recalled seeing Journey To The Center Of The Earth.

On the way home I was still feeling pretty good from the anesthetic, so I tried to get my wife to stop so I could buy her a diamond bracelet and a helicopter.

About a week after my colonoscopy I got a call from my doctor telling me that the tests on the polyp they removed were negative, and that my colon was in great shape. This was the best news I could hope for.

But then he went on to tell me that the way everything looked I wouldn't need another colonoscopy for ten years.

Darn. I was just getting the hang of it.

The BONEHED Theory of Devolution

Over the past year this column has become a rallying point for people interested in bringing our English language into the twenty-first century. In this spirit, we founded the very first chapter of the Bureau Of Nearly Everybody Hacking English Down, or BONEHED. Since then we have recruited BONEHEDs from throughout the English-bashing world.

As our first order of business, we've documented how text messaging has made enormous improvements in our language. For example, in days gone by a couple would have to end a romantic relationship with a speech like:

"Clyde, I just think we should see other people. Lots of people. In fact we should probably see everybody in the world except each other."

Part I: Bikes, Docks & Slush Nuggets

Now, modern communications technology has made it possible to accomplish this with a simple text message:

"I H8 U."

As every BONEHED knows, these marvelous changes haven't come overnight. There has been a long linguistic evolution that has brought us to this pinnacle of communication. For example, consider this comment from a guy about 300 years ago, hiding in the bushes outside a young girl's window:

Romeo: But soft! What light through yonder window breaks?

It is the East, and Juliet is the sun!

Arise, fair sun, and kill the envious moon

Who is already sick and pale with grief...

And it goes on and on like that. Don't you just want to grab this guy, shake him, and tell him to just get on with it, for crying out loud?

By the time I was in high school, communication was much improved. In the 1960s the guy in the bushes would say:

Romeo: Whoa! Look at the hot chick up on that balcony!

Officer Flannigan: All right, Peeping Tom, you have a right to remain silent...

Isn't that better? Of course, today Romeo

could just hold up his cell phone, take a quick picture, and disappear into the night.

Looking back, though, you have to admit that there have been some useful additions to the language over the past few years. There are a lot of words that just plain did not exist back when I was in high school. Of course, my son would be quick to point out that "fire" and "the wheel" didn't exist either back when I was in high school, but that would be a gross exaggeration. I had wheels on my chariot.

But think about it, it wasn't that long ago that we never said things like "Internet" or "E-mail." And if you mentioned any sort of "World Wide Web" your mom would have gone scrambling for a big broom and a can of Raid.

Back then we never heard of a PC, a CD, a VCR, a DVD, an iPod, or a GPS. We would have thought that a "blog" might be a big wet field where you planted cranberries.

Before October of 2001, if you said, "iPod," your wife would say, "Well, I hope you put the seat down."

And the meaning of words has evolved as well. At one time, a "pyramid" was something put together by the ancient Egyptians, not by your sister-in-law the Amway lady. I can even remember when a "thong" was a leather lace you bought for your hunting boot.

Being a die-hard Olympics junkie, I've also noticed significant changes in the language of sports. Just a few years ago there was no such thing as a "snowboard," and a "half pipe" was what you had after your friend "Badger" showed up at the party and sat on the "bong."

Finally, we should consider the effect of current culture on modern English. For example, one of the Olympic snowboarders finished his run in the half pipe with something called a "Switch Alley Oop Backside Rodeo." I didn't actually see the trick, but I just really, really hope it had nothing to do with Brokeback Mountain.

So there you have it, fellow BONEHEDs. Now it's up to you. Send your examples of the devolution of the English language to me at bonehed@learnedsofar.com.

Ask Dr. Mike – Relationships

In this week's column we're introducing a new feature; "Ask Dr. Mike," in which we explore topics relevant to life in today's complex society through genuine questions from genuine readers, none of which I made up – other than the readers' names, the questions, and the existence of the readers themselves. Ok, here goes:

Dear Dr. Funny Guy,

Why I ought to rip your arm off and beat you with the bloody stump.

I'd like to know the meaning of relationships and why I can't seem to get me any of 'em. All I really need in my life is a good woman to meet me at the door with my newspaper when I get home from a hard day at the office, stand by me no matter what kind of mood she may be in, and honor me forever with unconditional love and devotion. Is that too much to ask for?

You dirty commie.

Signed,

Plenty Of Love To Give

Well Plenty, it seems like what you're really looking for there is a cocker spaniel. I guess you might get a few women to go as far as that paper-at-the-door thing if you rub their bellies, but I wouldn't count on it. All in all, for you I'd recommend a trip to the animal shelter.

As for the meaning of relationships, this is something about which men have always been curious and women have always been angry. You see, we men have a hard time "relating" to another person, sharing thoughts and feelings, and forming deep emotional bonds. A woman can develop a long-term relationship with a bowl of Häagen-Dazs.

Good luck.

Dear Dr. Funny Guy,

Why I ought to rip your arm off and blah, blah, blah, blah.

I'm an almost unbelievably good-looking, intelligent guy with a great job, lots of money, and

What I've Learned So Far...

I drive a 'Vette. Why can't I seem to get any of the ignorant babes I meet to hook up with me in a long-term relationship?

You dirty blah, blah.

Signed,

Too-Good For Those Chicks, But Willing To Give Them A Break

Gosh Too-Good, I can't imagine why you would be having this problem. Maybe it's your haircut.

A long-term relationship between a man and a woman is a complicated thing. It can end up in marriage, or it can lead to a situation that experts like Dr. Laura might call "living in sin," which sounds like it would be a lot more interesting than marriage, but usually isn't. In either case, there are a few important relationship rules you should try to keep in mind.

First, let's consider the always-tricky issue of money. Just remember, her money is hers. She earned it, and she can damn well do anything she wants to with it.

Of course you should understand that your money is also hers. If you should happen to get some money, your best bet would be to hand it over to her immediately so she can give you some

Part I: Bikes, Docks & Slush Nuggets

back as an allowance. If you're good.

Second, never criticize her friends or family, no matter what. This is particularly important when she's telling you how awful they are. Just nod understandingly, or wrinkle your brow and shake your head, whichever seems appropriate.

By the same token, keep in mind that your friends are fundamentally no good. You're better off if you never talk to them or about them when she's around, and you should only see them when she's otherwise entertained. If you want to play some golf with the guys, buy her a DVD player and the first three seasons of Sex In The City.

Third, if she asks you for your opinion about anything pertaining to her, don't answer. I just can't stress this strongly enough. DON'T ANSWER! For instance, if she asks, "Do I look like I've gained weight?" just grab your jacket and leave. If you foolishly remain in the line of fire and say, "No Honey, of course not," she'll kick off the inevitable verbal death-spiral with something like, "So, you mean I've always been fat?"

If you find yourself cut off from an exit in this situation, you'll find that seizures, compound fractures, or strokes make nice alternatives.

Finally, when it comes to gifts, you can pretty much always assume that she means the opposite of what she says. If she tells you, "Oh, don't bother buying me anything for Sweetest Day," just smile, grab a credit card, and head for the mall.

Next week, we hear from the women.

Ask Dr. Mike
Relationships Episode 2: The Empress Strikes Back

Last week we introduced a new advice column feature in which we tackled the issue of relationships. By an astonishing coincidence, all the absolutely genuine (in the poetic sense) readers who wrote in were men asking for relationship advice, providing us with a sort of "premise" or "theme" for the piece.

This week, the women get to have their say.

Dear Dr. Funny Guy,

Why I ought to rip your arm off and beat you with the bloody stump.

I was deeply offended by your last column,

in which you said that a woman could develop a relationship with a bowl of Häagen-Dazs.

What a terrible generalization! Not this woman! I couldn't form a serious relationship with anything less than a full quart of Häagen-Dazs, and then it would have to be Rum Raisin.

Ok, maybe Butter Pecan.

Anyway, before we were married my husband bought me flowers, gave me nice gifts, and took me out to nice restaurants. These days his idea of a thoughtful romantic evening is trimming his toenails over a newspaper before the hockey game starts, so we can concentrate on whether the girl who sings the Star Spangled Banner is showing any cleavage. How do I get the old magic back?

Also, what kind of doctor are you?

You Saracen Pig.

Sincerely,

At Least He Uses A Newspaper

Well At, I'll answer the last question first. My degree is actually an honorary PhD bestowed on me by my college fraternity brothers. I'm fairly certain the PhD stands for "Phony Doctor," because there's a José Cuérvo label taped to the diploma. Hey, Dr. Laura's degree is in something like the History of Dry Cleaning, so that makes

Part I: Bikes, Docks & Slush Nuggets

me at least as qualified as she is to write this crap.

Now, before we delve into a deeply sensitive solution to your original problem, I need to ask you a question: Does the girl who sings the Star Spangled Banner before the hockey games really show cleavage sometimes? Wow, I'll have to check that out! I'm usually out making popcorn when she sings. Think of those high notes...

As for the "old magic," it's not really gone. It has just evolved from the enchanted blazing passion of young romance into the dying embers of two lives quietly slipping downward into a hopeless oblivion of broken dreams. And toenail clippings.

Just kidding, ha-ha. It's much worse than that!

One thing you could try that might add a little fuel to the fire would be to slip away during the last two minutes of that hockey game and come back as the horn blows, wearing nothing but a Steve Yzerman jersey and a coy smile. Who knows – you just might get a game misconduct.

Dear Dr. Funny Guy,

Why I ought to whatever your whatever off and whatever you with the bloody whatever.

My boyfriend wears enough cologne to teargas a medium-sized sectarian riot. Whenever he picks me up for a date he smells like an Old Spice truck crashed into the Aramis factory. What gives?

You running-dog capitalist swine.

Signed,

Getting Woozy With The Car Windows Closed

Well Woozy, I'm sorry to tell you that your boyfriend is what is clinically known as a "colognaholic."

I suspect that at some point in his life he splashed on a little after shave and then, as we say, "got lucky" – by which I (probably) mean that he found a quarter, made three stop lights in a row and won $7 on the lotto.

In his protozoan (male) mind he would naturally draw a parallel between the "scent" and the "luck," then come to the conclusion that the more of that stuff he slathered on, the luckier he'd get.

Of course most experts who have studied the colognaholic male relate the phenomenon to a deep-seated electrochemical imbalance common to the olfactory neural receptors of all men. In other words, guys' sniffers are all screwed up. This is why men can happily swap body odors and other mystery smells that would prove dangerous or lethal to most women.

Part I: Bikes, Docks & Slush Nuggets

If it makes you feel any better, Woozy, just look at the satisfied, even beatific look you see on your colognaholic's face when he is in "full-Brut." Most observers agree that it's identical to the ecstatic look a dog gets when he's been rolling in raccoon poop.

My advice to you is to relax and leave the car windows open. And just to be safe, keep your boyfriend away from places where raccoons have been hanging out. He is a guy, after all.

Ask Dr. Mike - Qualifications & More Questions

Over the past few weeks we've introduced a new feature in this column, called "Ask Dr. Mike," in which we tackle difficult real(ish) problems from genuine(ish) readers, with all the wisdom and insight that comes from years of writing hilarious(ish) jokes.

I should mention that my doctorate is actually a PhD (Phony Doctorate) in Bartending from the University of Tim On Line. Good old UTOL is a fine institution of higher education, and they'll be back to offering a full catalog of diplomas ($25 each, three for $60) in the fall once Tim completes his fifty hours of community service.

By incredible coincidence, our first letter addresses this very subject:

Dear Dr. Funny Guy,

Why I ought to rip your arm off and beat you with the bloody stump.

Exactly how does a PhD from the University of Tim qualify you to solve peoples' problems? You never show the professionalism that Dr. Laura or Dr. Phil do by viciously attacking people's feelings, beliefs or life choices. What are you, some kind of a wimp? How dare you condone people doing what they believe, instead of what I believe!

I was also wondering how I could have known about that University of Tim thing without reading the first two paragraphs of this column?

You commie fag junkie.

Your biggest fan,

A Pretty Implausible Reader

Gosh Pretty, thanks for writing me with those great questions.

First off, the exact title printed on the degree isn't everything. As I've pointed out before, Dr. Laura's PhD is in something like the Mechanics of Croquet which, now that I think of it, sort of explains why she isn't always completely in line with current psychological theory.

Dr. Phil actually has a degree in psychology, so I'm not sure what his excuse is.

Anyway, I just answer these questions as a regular guy, an average Joe – some might even say, a big palooka. This means that If I come up with an answer that is in any way useful or meaningful, it will either be a complete accident or a minor miracle.

As to your second question... I forgot what you asked. Sorry.

Dear Dr. Funny Guy,

Why I ought to stump your arm off and rip you with the bloody beat.

As a wife and mother, I was wondering what might be going on in the mind of a man when he is yelling at sports on television. Does he really think the players, the coaches or the refs can hear him?

Also, I think Pretty Implausible Reader was really mean to you, calling you a wimp. You can't help it if you're a kind and gentle person (a wimp). Instead, we should commend you for your tender good nature and sensitivity.

You scum-sucking pig

Sincerely,

Almost As Implausible

Gosh Almost, you bring up a good point when you ask what might be going on in the mind of a man. As a man myself I have to say that the odds are, not really all that much.

You see, we men are simple creatures. We respond to basic stimuli in a straightforward cycle of action and reaction, much like an amoeba pulling away from an electric shock, or a chemical industry lobbyist who wants to pollute the Colorado River voting Republican.

When we shout at the television, we are responding to primeval stimuli that urge us to respond this way to the situation. It all goes back to one caveman watching another fight a saber-tooth tiger. If the caveman watching was smart, he would watch from a distance. If he was *really* smart, he would watch from so far away that he couldn't be heard if he shouted – and he would shout just to make sure. Of these two cavemen, guess which one was around long enough to pass his genes down to the next generation?

So when modern man sits in his living room and screams at a 285 pound linebacker on television, he is simply trying to keep from being eaten by a saber-tooth tiger.

Well that's it for today. Be sure to send your life-changing questions to drmike@learnedsofar.com and post them there. I won't promise you that I'll always come up with helpful answers, but I will always try to make up something that sounds convincing.

More or less.

Ask Dr. Mike - Sea Monkeys, Colors & Skidmarks

Over the past few weeks we've introduced a new feature, called "Ask Dr. Mike." Here at last is your big chance to share your innermost thoughts, feelings and ideas with a guy who writes jokes for a living!

Good luck with that.

Now you may very well ask, "Is this Dr. Mike guy qualified to solve my problems? Is he a licensed counselor? Is he Freudian or Jungian? Does he believe in dream analysis? Boxers or briefs? What's that green stuff on his shirt?"

Boy, would you ever be nosey! But in the spirit of full disclosure, I'll be happy to answer all of your questions:

Not really.

No.

A who-ian?

Sure, why not?

Boxers.

And, what green stuff?

Now I should point out that much like Dr. Laura, who has her doctorate in something like Theoretical fruit pickling, my postgraduate degree does not exactly make me a psychotherapist. My PhD is actually a Phony Doctorate in bartending from the University of Tim On Line. To those of you who are going to go all "academic" on me and claim that my doctorate is not even worth the $20 I paid for it, I say, "Oh yeah?"

Actually, I look back with fond memories of the half hour or so that I spent in the ivy-covered Web pages of good old UTOL, filling out the credit card form, picking out my preferred diploma style, and thinking up a title for my doctoral thesis:

Sea Monkeys: Anthropomorphic Phenomenon, or Goldfish Food?

Ok, so let's get down to our first letter:

Dear Dr. Funny Guy,

Why I ought to rip your arm off and beat you with the bloody stump.

Part I: Bikes, Docks & Slush Nuggets

So what's the deal with women and colors? It seems like they're always worried about subtleties of what matches which, and what goes together with who, and why you shouldn't wear your pea-green "Oasis" t-shirt with your favorite maroon Bermuda shorts and mustard socks.

I mean, they just don't get the concept of individual style. You show up to take them to the Turnip Festival and they act all nauseated about what you're wearing.

On a related note, do you know a good way to get barf stains out of an Oasis t-shirt?

You pond scum.

Your pal,

Pretty Sure I'm An "Autumn"

Well Pretty, first off, from the way you describe your wardrobe, I'm guessing that you're probably living in the basement of your parents' house. This would mean that you're never too far from the dumpster. I'd advise you to throw all your clothes in that dumpster and start going naked. Before you know it you'll be wearing those nice bright orange jail coveralls. As for what women think – well, that won't be an issue for the next 2-5 years.

Thanks for writing.

What I've Learned So Far...

We have time for one more letter:

Dear Dr. Funny Guy,

Why I ought to rip your arm off and do whatever it is everybody else likes to do to you.

My husband just came home from an auction, having bought a wood lathe, a jack hammer, and an arc welding kit, and told me that he was going into business for himself making solid oak lawn mowers. But that's not what I'm writing you about.

What can I do about handling my husband's dirty underwear? Last month a seal ruptured in my hazmat suit and I was found three days later, slumped over the utility sink. I'd probably still be there if the gas meter-reader had not wandered into the laundry room.

And don't tell me to have him do the laundry himself. The last time he tried that it took a week to rescue the neighbors from the roofs of their homes, and FEMA is now telling us that the ultimate restoration of our neighborhood may take another year. I need your advice – Help!

You rancid bag of dog kibbles.
Sincerely,
Other Than That He's The Perfect Man

Gosh Other, that's a tough one. We men

Part I: Bikes, Docks & Slush Nuggets

take a certain amount of pride in our ability to turn pretty much any item of clothing into toxic waste – especially our underwear. Your husband sounds like an extreme case, medically known as skidmarkius maximus. Whatever you do, you want to avoid damaging his delicate – if smelly – self image.

The way I see it, the real problem here is your cheap hazmat suit. My advice would be to apply to the EPA and have your laundry room declared a Superfund cleanup site, so you can bring in professional equipment.

Goodbye Brenna

Yesterday Nan and I had to do one of the hardest things a person ever has to do. We said goodbye to Brenna the Dog.

If you've read my column for any length of time, you probably know about Brenna. She was, in my opinion, the best dog that it is possible for a dog to be.

But then I might be a little bit biased.

Brenna was ten years old. This is pretty ancient for a Doberman, but she still had the strong spark of a puppy in her. She was fanatically curious, interested in everything – although, like all dogs, her interest grew even more intense if a particular everything promised to involve food. And if you'd ever met her you would know that she loved every living creature.

Except maybe squirrels.

Part I: Bikes, Docks & Slush Nuggets

It seems that Brenna had an inoperable tumor at the top of her lungs that had been growing, unnoticed, for some time. Nevertheless, she was the picture of health, and I even had the hubris recently to blather quite a bit about what great shape she was in for a Dobie her age.

A couple of weeks ago that tumor suddenly shifted. It began to push against her windpipe, making it more and more difficult for her to breathe. For a while she still seemed completely fine, just coughing occasionally as if she had swallowed something that probably would have been better off un-swallowed.

But by yesterday the problem had progressed to the point that if she tried to lie down, or even sit, the tumor would shut off her air almost completely and slowly strangle her.

So she stood in the middle of the room, as still as she could, gasping for breath. And as she stood there she looked at me with a look of puzzled misery on her face that I'd never seen before.

It was nothing like the "begging-for-a-handout" look, or the "yoo-hoo-I-gotta-pee" look, or the "I-had-a-little-accident-in-the-other-room" look, or even the "how-about-shoving-a-knuckle-in-my-right-ear-because-that-would-probably-feel-good" look.

I knew that she was saying, "I'm not quite sure what's happening to me, but I could use a little help here." And as much as I tried to deny the reality of the situation, I knew that helping her was my job.

I have to say that for the eight years Brenna was with us, I tried really hard to repay the unconditional, limitless love that she just gave out naturally, every minute of our lives together. And I also have to say that I don't believe I was ever able to even come close. So I guess the best I could do was to be willing to face up to my duty yesterday when the time came.

I do find comfort in knowing that the last thing Brenna knew in this world was the touch of my hand scratching her ears, and the sound of my voice reminding her that I loved her.

And to prove it, my tears.

Part I: Bikes, Docks & Slush Nuggets

Pondering Peeps

Well, it's Easter. This weekend commemorates the sacrifice that Jesus Christ made for all of us when he was crucified, suffered, and died for the sins of all mankind, then rose and ascended into heaven. So how do Americans celebrate the holiest event in the Christian calendar?

With Peeps.

For those of you who have been living off-planet, Peeps are those yellow marshmallow chicks that you see at Easter time. And I say, what more appropriate way could there be to celebrate the holy Resurrection than eating cute little baby waterfowl made out of sugar-coated... sugar?

Now I may be wrong, but I don't think Peeps have ever really been embraced as part of any holiday besides Easter. It seems logical that the Peep people would have probed the possibilities of

Poltergeist Peeps for Halloween, Pilgrim Peeps for Thanksgiving, or Pére Noel Peeps for Christmas. They may have even tried out Patriot Peeps for the Fourth of July.

But the proper yellow Peeps, and to a lesser extent the preposterously progressive Purple Peeps, have remained primarily in the purview of Easter.

True, there are Easter food traditions besides Peeps. For generations, milk chocolate rabbits have traumatized small children by posing one of their earliest and most critical life decisions; ears-down, or feet-up?

I'm an ears-down man myself, but I'm still working through my guilt issues over years of unrepentantly biting the head off the Easter Bunny.

Then there are Easter Eggs. I know all about how the egg symbolizes birth or beginning, as in Spring or the Resurrection itself. I'm just not real sure how painting them up in bright colors, hiding them, then staging a full-contact preschool Oklahoma Land Rush to find them fits into that metaphor.

And I've always kind of wondered about the tradition of the Easter Ham. Doesn't it seem a little peculiar to serve up the old Honey Baked hog brisket in honor of Jesus - who was a rabbi?

Just asking.

Part I: Bikes, Docks & Slush Nuggets

One interesting thing about Peeps is that I don't think very many of them actually get eaten on Easter Sunday. Like a fine wine, you have to let a Peep "breathe" before you consume it. As any Peep purist knows, Peeps are particularly palatable if you poke perforations in the Peep package, then wait an appropriate period until they reach their chewy, palate-pleasing prime.

Don't you suppose those progressively alliterative Peeps are perhaps a pretty paltry premise for publishing these palpably non-polemic paragraphs?

Probably. Profound apologies, people.

A Tribute To Masters Hockey

A while back, this column featured a primer on youth ice hockey. As I write this, the NHL Playoffs are just getting into full swing. And they are bound to keep on swinging, landing some pretty good blows, until sometime late in June. With this in mind, I thought I'd take this opportunity to tell you a little bit about the grown-up side of the game.

All kinds of adults play ice hockey, including many who are my age and older. This is possible because as we mature and our bodies become more injury-prone, we also progressively lose our mental competence. By the time a player is as old as I am, it's a miracle if he can remember which part of the shoulder pads to stick his head through, much less enjoy the good sense to stay off the ice.

Part I: Bikes, Docks & Slush Nuggets

Now in the column about youth hockey, I pointed out that there is a sort of "Talent Inverse-Square Rule" we use for naming player levels - the higher the skill level, the more demeaning the name. The biggest, fastest, hardest-hitting young players short of the professional leagues are called "Midgets." Partly in deference to this Inverse-Square Rule, and partly because we are the ones who make up the names, we older hockey players are called "Masters."

Masters hockey games generally happen late at night, when ice time is cheap, and when the rink manager overlooks the coolers of beer in the locker room because he is either asleep or thirsty.

People rarely come to watch Masters games, and for years I wondered why. After all, as far as we are concerned our games feature all the blinding speed of the NHL, coupled with the keen play and finesse that comes naturally to us as more mature, experienced athletes. Despite this, inviting our wives or long-term significant others to our games generally has about the same effect as inviting them to eat a bucket of gravel.

One night a few years back, my team actually did have a spectator. She was, predictably, the New Girlfriend of our only single player, and even more exciting than her presence, she had brought along a video camera.

What I've Learned So Far...

What a game! Waiting for the opening face-off, I could feel the lens capturing my scowl of concentration as I watched the puck in the referee's hand, coiled to pounce like a panther the instant he dropped it.

All night long we flew up and down the ice like blazing comets. Every pass I fired across the rink cracked with deafening authority onto the blade of my teammate's stick, and every pass I received cracked with that same authority. Late in the game I even scored a highlight-reel goal, rifling the puck past the catching glove of the desperately lunging goalie.

And New Girlfriend got it all on tape.

After the game, and after we polished off all the beer in the locker room, someone pointed out that one of our favorite bars was still open, and that they had a large-screen TV... WITH A VCR!

Trembling with excitement we swilled the first pitcher or two while the bartender cued up our video. Finally, following a few seconds of shaky footage of New Girlfriend's shoes and a few helpful shouts from the other bar patrons of, "Hey what's this crap?" our sports epic began.

The opening face-off wasn't exactly as I remembered it. After the referee dropped the puck, the players up on the screen stood around motionless on the ice for what seemed like a very

Part I: Bikes, Docks & Slush Nuggets

long time while the old guy wearing a jersey with my number on it and the opposing center stood there and looked at it, apparently discussing what to do next.

Eventually we came to some sort of conclusion and began swatting at the puck, knocking it in the general direction of the penalty box. All ten players ambled off in that general direction, and the game was on.

After we all took turns asking New Girlfriend and the bartender if they were certain the tape was running at the right speed, and being assured that it was, the entire team settled back to let the cruel tide of VHS Reality wash over us.

We watched those "blazing comets" shuffling up and down the ice in glacial clusters, sometimes with the puck but more often chasing it. The deafening crack of those pinpoint passes never once made it to the sound track, completely drowned out by our wheezing and New Girlfriend's occasional giggles. And my highlight-reel goal amounted to the puck bouncing lazily off my stick and trickling past the goalie while he was looking at a loose strap on one of his pads.

Now I have to say that I think NHL players are among the finest all-around athletes in the world, and that watching them play hockey is to see the game as it was meant to be played. And I also have to say that until I actually saw my team up on that screen, I had believed that we Masters were just enjoying an ever-so-slightly more deliberate and cerebral version of the same sport.

Well, we do use black rubber pucks...

A Truck?

I just got off the phone with my son. He's twenty-four years old, he's not sick, and he doesn't need money (at least not from me). Under these circumstances a call from him pretty much ranks right up there with a call from the Pope.

"So, what's up?" I asked, figuring that if His Holiness needed to get hold of me he would just have to make do with my voice mail.

"Well," my son said, "I'm shopping for a new truck."

"A truck?" I replied. "Why?"

"What do you mean, 'Why?'"

"I mean, 'Why?' as in, have you taken up carpentry? Or ranching? You work in an office and live in an apartment. So tell me, why would you need a truck?"

"People always need trucks."

"Carpenters and ranchers do."

"What if I was going to move? I'd need the truck to haul all my stuff."

"Are you going to move any time soon?"

"No. But one of my friends might."

"Why can't they buy their own truck?"

"Don't be stupid."

"Sorry, I don't know what came over me. So what kind of truck are you looking at?"

"A Petro-Slurp 250, with a Twin-overhead Something and a Turbo Otherthing."

"That sounds expensive."

"Not really. In fact, I'll actually save money."

"How do you figure?"

"Well, first off, it will be cheaper than fixing my car."

"Does your car need fixing?"

"Well, no. But it will. Eventually. Probably."

"If you were to put as much as the truck payment into that car every month, you could replace everything, including the ashtray, in less than a year."

"You're just not seeing the big picture."

"Apparently not. So what about fuel

economy? That Petro-Slurp is going to burn some gas."

"Actually, the gas mileage is almost as good as I get in the car."

"Doesn't your car get about twenty-five miles per gallon?"

"Well, yeah."

"And the truck gets, what, eight?"

"Nearly eight and a quarter. Going downhill. With a tail wind."

"So the truck uses just about three times as much gas."

"See, that's not all that much different."

"Yeah, at almost three bucks a gallon, you'll hardly notice."

"Plus, I have my motorcycle. I can always save gas by using that to drive back and forth to work."

"True. That will be a particularly attractive option in the eight months a year that have "r" in them."

"There are usually some decent bike days in September and April."

"True enough. It's good to see that you've done your homework."

"Besides, what do you care what I spend?"

"Hey, I spent a third of my life saving up to put you through a good college. Now it's your turn to save up to put me in a good nursing home."

"See, there's another good thing about the truck - I can use it to move you into the nursing home."

"Well, I wasn't planning on doing that for at least a few more weeks. Anyway, it sounds like you've pretty much made up your mind."

"Yeah, I guess so."

"Ok, so what are you calling me for?"

"I just needed to hear your opinion."

I smiled away the lump in my throat. "Son, my opinion is, if it makes sense to you and you're sure you can afford it, then you should go for it."

"I knew you were going to say that, sooner or later."

"Yeah, so did I. Do you need to hear my opinion on anything else?"

"Not right now. Bye Dad."

"So long, Son."

The Circle of Crap

New leaf-buds erupt on every tree in a riot of impossible green. Flowers spread their newborn blossoms to kiss the gentle rain. Pasty-white legs poke tentatively out of creased shorts that smell like mothballs.

It's Spring!

Here in the Midwest there is an even more reliable sign of spring, usually seen scrawled with a magic marker on flaps torn from brown corrugated cardboard boxes. And the sign says:

"RUMMAGE SALE."

While I've never actually looked it up, I can say with some authority that I know what "Rummage" means. It means "Crap." And I'm willing to bet that the word was invented by someone who had the good marketing sense to understand the down-side of a sign that said,

What I've Learned So Far...

"CRAP SALE."

Nevertheless, a Rummage Sale is a place where people go to get or get rid of Crap. In fact, it's not at all unusual to see a person bring some Crap in and take different Crap home. This is all part of the natural flow of life that I like to call the "Circle of Crap."

The first part of the Circle is mankind's obsessive and never-ending Quest for Crap. This is the same primal urge that moves a teenager to get his first job, or Attila the Hun to pillage Europe – in both cases they are just trying to accumulate more Crap than they had before.

Once you get yourself some Crap, you need to take care of it. Consider that at the most basic level all you really need in the way of a "home" is some way to keep your body warm. Anything beyond that is about your Crap. You get a roof and walls to keep your Crap dry, you put doors in the walls so you can get to your Crap, and you put locks on those doors so other people can't.

As you gather more and more Crap, you need more and more space to keep it in, and this added space can become highly specialized. You might have a Garage for your Rolling Crap, a Kitchen for your Edible Crap, and a Family Room for your Family Crap.

Inevitably though, from almost the instant

you get your Crap, and even though you continue to put a lot of effort into taking care of it, you begin to lose interest in it. Before you've paid the Visa bill off you are often casting your covetous eyes on newer, better, more up-to-date Crap.

As your desire for new Crap grows, so does your dissatisfaction with the Crap you already have, and you begin to think of it as "Old Crap." Before long you're finding excuses not to use your Old Crap, and you eventually demote it to storage in the Attic, the Basement or the Garage.

While moving Old Crap to storage theoretically opens you up to bringing in some New Crap, this is a temporary solution at best. In fact, if you were raised in a guilt-based environment (in other words, if you are anything like me), you may find it hard to go out and buy New Crap when you have essentially the same Old Crap sitting in the garage and keeping your Rolling Crap parked out in the driveway.

So you decide to get rid of the Old Crap. But since you might still remember when your Old Crap was New Crap you just can't bring yourself to simply throw it away, to wind up in some landfill covered with dirt and other peoples' Crap.

Finally, driven by a blend of desperation and nostalgia, you look for something useful to do with your Old Crap. Life would be perfect if only you could find someone to whom it could become, even for a while, New Crap.

The solution, of course, is the Rummage Sale. Your old Crap becomes someone else's new Crap, you don't have to deal with the old Crap any more, and you get money you can put toward some newer and better Crap of your own.

And so the Circle of Crap is complete.

God Bless America!

Part I: Bikes, Docks & Slush Nuggets

Mother's Day

All right guys, Sunday is Mother's Day. Yellow alert! Go to DefCon 1!

For those of you who are not familiar with A.D.S.D. (Association of Dads, Sons and Daughters) nomenclature, DefCon refers to situations in which failing to live up to Mom's expectations will result in Definite Consequences.

For example, forgetting to take out the garbage on pickup day might take us to DefCon 4, Definite Consequences of the 4th degree, meaning that a mild scolding is in the offing. Failure to mow the lawn or perform some other assigned task would be considered DefCon 3 infractions, with correspondingly greater consequences, while coming home from Chuck E. Cheese's with one less (or more) kid than we left home with will get us instantly and uncomfortably into DefCon 2 territory.

In the three basic DefCon 1 situations - her birthday, your anniversary and Mother's Day - failure is simply not an option.

The idea of Mother's Day has been around in this country since just after the Civil War, when Julia Ward Howe (who wrote the words to the Battle Hymn of the Republic) issued her Mother's Day Peace Proclamation. Since then we've put Julia on a stamp, brought in the Hallmark people, and pretty much got rid of that pesky old "Peace" thing that was cluttering up her idea.

So now we set aside one Sunday each year to honor the Moms of the world. We might start out the day by making her breakfast in bed, treating her to a succulent banquet of chocolate chip waffles and orange juice. And if we're careful in the kitchen, it won't take her much more than four or five hours to clean up after us.

Of course we should also get Mom a present, something thoughtful yet fun, something that will appeal to her romantic nature. The big gift idea this season is the Sucks-Much XXL Vacuum Cleaner. It comes with the "Chiropractor's Friend" attachment package – an assortment of tubes, funny-looking plastic things and brushes that fit into a compartment on the handle and kick the curb weight up to about 215 pounds.

Part I: Bikes, Docks & Slush Nuggets

And then there's the Mother's Day card. You need to find her something sentimental yet cheerful, with a deeply spiritual message. Something like:

Mom, you're beautiful and fragrant;

You've helped us grow from boys to men.

Without you, Dad would be a vagrant;

Oops, the cat puked in the Den.

You know, while Mother's Day does put a certain amount of pressure on all us Dads, Sons and Daughters, it seems to me that giving the Moms of this world their own special day is well worth the effort. How can we really thank the woman who was the primary diaper changer, nose wiper, Band-Aid applier, playground supervisor, educational consultant, nutritional expert, transportation facilitator, recreation coordinator, and Dad pacifier in our young lives.

And as Dads, how can we even begin to repay the woman who is all of those things for our children.

Of course there are a lot of people like me whose mother might still be looking after us, only she's doing it from somewhere up above. We can't send her a card or hand her a bouquet of flowers. The best we can do is hold her in our hearts and smile – didn't she always love to see you smile?

What I've Learned So Far...

So how can we really show our gratitude to someone who, for most of her adult life, has quietly accepted the idea that all the things she wanted would come in a distant second to all the things that might just make her family happier?

How about saying, "I Love You Mom. Thanks for everything."

Part I: Bikes, Docks & Slush Nuggets

Ask Dr. Mike - Still More Words of Wisdom

It's time for another installment of "Ask Dr. Mike," in which readers entrust their most important problems to a doofus who writes jokes for a living.

Dear Dr. Funny Guy,

Why I ought to rip your arm off and beat you with the bloody stump.

I thought that my husband and I had finally arrived at the perfect marriage – I hadn't seen him in nearly two months, but the paychecks kept coming in. Now it turns out that all that time he was lost in the basement, somewhere between the furnace and the water softener.

We've had this problem before, beginning right

after we got married when he disappeared for two days trying to find the bathroom in the honeymoon suite. Last Christmas I bought him a portable GPS that had key locations – his job, his best friend's house, the kitchen – programmed in, but he just won't use it.

What gives?

You trash-picking sleaze.

Sincerely,

Oh Crap, He's Missing Again

Well Crap, as every psychologist and stand-up comic in history has pointed out (repeatedly), we men all suffer from a disorder known as "Stopandaskophobia."

We can trace this syndrome back to the Middle Ages, when a wanderer might pause in his journey along the dusty road to ask directions from a farmer laboring in the field. "Prithee, stout yeoman," he would say, "Canst thou direct me to the corner of St. George Street and Dragon Ave?"

To which the peasant would traditionally reply, "My name is not 'Stout Yeoman,' it's 'Steve,' and do I looketh like bloody AAA to you?" Then he would stab our traveler with his pitchfork.

As you might imagine, the average pilgrim soon learned that he was probably better off just to wing it when it came to finding his way around the Middle Ages.

Moving ahead to the present time, it was initially believed that the invention of the GPS would pretty much eliminate Stopandaskophobia among modern men. Surely no guy would have a problem with getting directions from a little electronic box!

Of course as we now know, this hope was crushed, and those age-old genetic memories immediately resurfaced, when we found out that "GPS" really stood for "Grab a Pitchfork, Steve."

As for how to deal with your husband, my advice would be to staple one of those radio tracking devices to his ear – for availability simply contact your local National Geographic adventure show host. Then at least you can follow his migration patterns.

Good luck!

Dear Dr. Funny Guy,

I have two questions for you. First, exactly why does everybody who writes to you want to rip your arm off and beat you with the bloody stump? This seems highly aggressive and violent to me - although I also find it to be a surprisingly appealing idea.

Second, do you believe anxieties are sublimated or even ameliorated through the involuntary expression of psychosomatic phenomena, and do you think this in turn addresses some sort of anthropological imperative in the lives of modern homo sapiens?

You flatulent offspring of an Australopithecus.

Inquisitively,

Maybe A Little Too Much Time On My Hands To Think About This Stuff

You know Hands, I've often wondered about that myself. The first thing I mean, the arm ripping and the beating with the bloody stump.

I think the implied anger may simply be a reflection of the whole idea of me being an internationally known columnist. If you consistently write hard-hitting, insightful analysis of important issues, you're bound to antagonize a few people. If, like me, you go the next step and get paid to simply put random words on paper, you'll piss off just about everybody.

As to your second question, I can only say sure, anthropological imperative and stuff.

Why not?

A Guide For Grill Guys

As I have probably made all too clear in the past, I love my grill.

Admittedly, this statement coming from an American male is about as shocking as saying, "When it comes to breathing, I find that I lean toward air." But there it is - I'm a dedicated "grill guy."

This is not a new thing. In prehistoric times, a typical Hunter-Gatherer might come home from a hard day's H&G-ing, dragging, let's say, a woolly mammoth. Right away, his wife would want to chop it up, dump cream of mushroom soup on it, cover it with those nasty little onion rings, and make it into a casserole.

Now anybody who knows about casseroles can tell you that this is a lady's dish, maybe just the thing for her bridge club or cave-painting group, but not really what a guy wants to sink his teeth into after getting home from a hard day of scrubbing the woolly mammoth guts off his best spear. So our ancestor would take his catch outside, fire up an acre or two of savannah, and broil himself a mess of real big steaks.

Over the course of millions of years of evolution, this routine has become imprinted right into our genetic code. Researchers at the prestigious Ann Arbor Institute for Explaining Guy Stuff To Your Wife recently identified an area on the "Y" chromosome that scientists call the "Open Pit" gene. In experiments involving splicing this gene into lab mice, they discovered that unless you allow the genetically-altered little fellows to go out in the back yard to sear packages of tiny bratwursts, they soon lose the will to live.

But history and genetics aside, we men have to realize that it is our fatherly duty to pass on to our sons the lore of the grill. Imagine the tragedy of a generation of young men who don't know how to singe their eyebrows in a grease fire while they drink beer and discuss lawn care products with a neighbor.

A truly comprehensive set of grilling dos-and-don'ts would be beyond the scope of this column, since that would require me to do some actual research. However, here are a few major things that every young man should know.

First, pick a grill with lots of heating power. The standard unit of heat for a grill is the BTU (Burns Things Up). One BTU is computed as a fraction of the amount of heat it takes to turn an average hamburger into a charcoal briquette. As with most things in a man's life, bigger automatically means better, so you'll want a grill that will produce as many BTUs as you can afford. Rich guys have grills that will melt titanium.

Speaking of charcoal briquettes, there are a few die-hards out there who still believe in cooking over charcoal , instead of gas. The down side of these old-style grills is that you have to haul charcoal, light it, wait for it to reach the right temperature, and clean out the ashes when you're finished. The up side is that you get the fun of playing with charcoal lighter fluid (experts strongly discourage lighting your charcoal with "unauthorized" substances like gasoline or napalm).

All in all, I'll stick with propane or natural gas.

Here in the twenty-first century, you want your grill to display as much stainless steel as possible. I have no idea how this would benefit your cooking, but it should really impress your friends. It might even make the grill itself last longer, although considering the inevitable propane or natural gas explosions you're bound to be setting off, that's probably a moot point.

Finally, you need to develop a little grill-guy showmanship. For example, if your pork chop catches on fire and you dump your beer on it, you will not only put out the fire, but as an added bonus you get to immediately go and grab yourself a new, much colder beer. But always tell your friends that they just witnessed your "secret family recipe," and swear them to silence.

Never use an actual recipe, though, secret family or otherwise. You may consider this the Prime Directive of grill-guy cooking. If your repertoire is any more complicated than dumping in some seasoned salt and an occasional beer – well, you might as well be making a casserole.

Ugh!

Part I: Bikes, Docks & Slush Nuggets

Who Needs A Prenup?

This afternoon I was talking to my friends Josh and Cliff, and the conversation naturally turned to Paul McCartney's breakup with Heather Mills. Ok, I'm willing to admit that this may only be natural for three guys who all follow different spectator sports, who don't hunt or play golf, and are too married and too old to chase women. Trust me, none of us reads People magazine. Really.

Well, I do. But just for the ads.

Anyway, Cliff mentioned that the unpleasantness between Sir Paul and Lady Heather was made worse by the lack of a prenuptial agreement - worse to the tune of about $200 million out of Paul's hard-earned stash, leaving him to make do with just a little less than $700 million.

Well, needless to say, we were outraged! A

couple more blunders like that and the old Beatle would be reduced to buying his foie gras at Costco!

And that got us thinking about our own situations. It turns out that the one (and only) thing we all have in common with Paul McCartney is the lack of a prenuptial agreement. So a little later when I got home I found my wife sitting in the living room reading a book, and I said, "Honey, I think we should get a prenup."

"A what?"

"A prenup – you know, a prenuptial agreement. It's a document that spells out in detail how we're going to handle the finances in our marriage."

She turned the page. "Did you hit your head on the dryer vent again?"

"Not yet today. And I'm serious, we need a prenup."

"'Prenuptial' means 'before marriage.' We've been married 31 years."

"I should really consider protecting the assets I brought into this relationship. I don't know what I could have been thinking."

"You brought a guitar and an old Volkswagen microbus into this relationship. And, I'm pretty sure, that t-shirt you have on."

"And what about our son?"

"He didn't even have a guitar when he came out - something I've always been thankful for."

I could see that this was going to require an approach steeped in fiscal logic. "So how about all the assets we've accumulated?"

"Yeah, that is a real problem. We'd have to take out a loan to pay for a book about how to write a prenup, which should tell you something about all those assets we've accumulated."

"How about that annuity thingy we put away for retirement?"

"We spent that last month, fixing the door latch on the dishwasher."

"Oh yeah." I was getting frustrated. "Look, Josh told me that Heather offered to sign a prenup, and Paul turned her down, and now here he is up to his keister in Costco foie gras!"

"You did too hit your head on the dryer vent."

Just then the phone rang. It was Josh. "So," he said, "Have you talked your wife into signing a prenup yet?"

"Not yet. Any luck on your end?"

"Well no, but I've been informed that I'm about ten words away from moving my assets into the garage."

"How do you know that?"

"Because that's what she just told me."

"Ten words away from moving your assets into the garage? Wow!" I looked at my wife, who smiled back at me and held up five fingers.

Ok, I guess we can do without that prenup.

Do We Really Want To Speak English?

Earlier this year the United States Senate passed a resolution declaring English the official language of this country. It seems that our great nation has never actually had an official language of its own before.

Wow! Hooray for the Red, White and Blue! At long last, our people will be united under a common set of nouns, verbs, adjectives, adverbs, and yes, even the occasional gerund. We'll all speak English!

So when do we start?

"Hey, wait just a garsh danged minute here," you may say, "I done been talking English all my life! And stuff!"

Well, Bucko, I hate to be the one to break it

What I've Learned So Far...

to you, but whatever it is we've been "talking" all our lives here in America falls a bit on the "not so much" side of what our British cousins consider the mother tongue. The language we actually speak in these here parts is "American."

The difference between "American" and "English" is simple - "American" generally involves using a whole lot fewer words. Entire British phrases like, "I'm terribly sorry, but could you possibly repeat that?" or "I would be eternally grateful if you would be so kind as to elucidate that last point," are replaced in American with the elegant and versatile, "Huh?"

Now while American may not be universally considered the Language of The Bard, it could arguably be called the Language of the Lard. We are obsessed with consumption, and so when it comes to food, our national lexicon is rich and varied.

Americans have more words for "hamburger" than Inuits have for "snow*." We have the "Big Mac," the "Steakburger," the "Quarter Pounder" (with and without cheese), the "Patty Melt," the "Whopper," the "Hot & Juicy," the "Blimpy Burger" (found at Krazy Jim's, at the corner of Packard and Division for you non-Ann Arborites), the "Insert-Name-Of-Bar-Here Burger," and the very aptly (if nauseatingly) named "Slider."

Part I: Bikes, Docks & Slush Nuggets

Apparently accuracy is not all that important in the culinary segment of the American language. "Hamburgers" have nothing to do with ham, "French fries" have nothing to do with France, and "hot dogs" have (I really hope) nothing to do with dogs.

There are many other instances in which "American" is very different from "English." In English, "football" involves thin people in shorts sprinting around on a huge green field of grass, bouncing incredibly hard white volleyballs off their heads, and falling to the ground, writhing in agony, if another thin person in shorts happens to brush up against their jersey.

In American, "football" means gigantic men in full armor repeatedly crashing head-to-head into each other until they are either unconscious or crippled, while pretty girls in skimpy costumes dance around on the sidelines.

Now that's a sport!

So Senate, let's be clear on what we are trying to accomplish here. The way your legislation reads, if we're going to speak English we're all going to need to learn completely new meanings for words like "torch," "bonnet," "chips," "lift," "kidney pie," and "blimey."

On second thought, it might be best if you did not, to paraphrase George W. Bush, "misunderestimate our own rich culturizational heritage." Yes, it might just be that there is really only one choice for the official language here in the United States of America:

American.

The commonly repeated adage that the Inuit people have anywhere from 150 to 400 words for "snow" turns out to be a myth. They actually have five or six words describing different kinds of snow, about the same as we have in English. All those other words turn out to be variations on the phrase, "Those People From The South Are A Bunch Of Gullible Meatheads."

Getting A New Cell Phone - A Walk On The Wild Side

I got a new cell phone last week.

Ok, it's true that my old cell phone was working perfectly, did everything I needed, and even had a bunch of features on it that I still hadn't figured out how to use. It's just that every two years my cell phone company gives me a new one for free - meaning that the price I pay for service is so exorbitant that they can afford to do that. So you see, it was really just a matter of carefully weighing all the economic subtleties of the situation and making the rational decision to take the new phone.

That, and like most men, I'm attracted to shiny objects.

My wife also got a new phone. She didn't

really want to, but she had used her old phone as a tack hammer once too often, and for the past six months her contact list had been displaying all of the entries in Cantonese. She decided that getting a new phone was easier than taking the Cantonese language classes.

So we went down to the cell phone store and handed our phones over to a clerk wearing a black World Of WarCraft t-shirt under his white dress shirt and clip-on necktie. He explained our options to us and patiently answered insightful questions like, "Will this phone do any better than the old one if I accidentally drop it in the blender with the margaritas?"

My wife picked out a model that looked as much like her old phone as possible, on the theory that if it looked the same it should work the same, and that would make it easier for her to set up and use. The clerk, struggling to stifle his laughter, handed her the new phone and a five-pound stack of user manuals.

I, on the other hand, was in the mood for a change. I wanted to move up to the newest technology, experiencing the very latest developments in the exciting world of wireless telecommunications. After careful consideration, I chose a "Razr."

Part I: Bikes, Docks & Slush Nuggets

This thing is pretty cool. Despite the name, I haven't figured out yet how to shave with it, but I can download and listen to whole albums of music. I can do email and text-messages. I can browse the Web. My Razr has a built-in video camera so I can shoot still pictures and home movies. It has a calendar, alarm clock, world clock, notepad, calculator, and (this is absolutely true) a Global Positioning System. I can, for a price, download entire movies to enjoy on my Razr's giant 1-inch color screen.

If I want to, I can even use it to make and receive phone calls.

My Razr came with a Bluetooth wireless headset. You've seen these things; they hang in your ear and let you use the phone without ever touching it. My Bluetooth headset is comfortable, it works fine, and the calls sound great on both ends. The only down side is that it has a large flashing blue light on it, so when I'm using it I look like I am about to say, "Resistance is futile!" and then assimilate everyone around me into the Borg collective.

If you didn't understand that last Star Trek - The Next Generation reference, it's not really worth looking up. And if you did get it, I'll bet you can tell me where I can buy myself a World of WarCraft t-shirt.

What I've Learned So Far...

Programming A New Cell Phone
The Agony And More Agony

In last week's column we talked about how my wife and I picked out new cell phones. As I'm sure you recall, this was a process only slightly more complicated than planning and executing a space shuttle launch.

The real fun began after we got home. At the store, the cell phone guy had showed us how to set up and personalize our new phones with quick, confident keystrokes, ending the demonstration with the sanguine instruction, "You just follow the menus – it's simple."

So we sat down in our living room with our new phones, fully believing that we would spend no more than a few minutes unleashing all the powerful features that have become essential to modern communications; caller ID, call timers,

Part I: Bikes, Docks & Slush Nuggets

global 911 tracking, and customized ring tones that can make your phone sound like a Munchkin belching the Star Spangled Banner.

You know, you would think that by this point in my life I would have learned that hearing the word "simple" pretty much guarantees that whatever it refers to is not. We spent the next three days sitting side by side on the couch, generating a steady chorus of clicks, beeps, and the occasional Munchkin belch, breaking only for a few sips of water or a granola bar. Finally my wife dropped her phone on the coffee table in despair and croaked, "Have you figured out how to set the screen-saver?"

"No," I replied, "but don't worry about that right now. I think I just accidentally deactivated our bank accounts and triggered a NATO invasion of Syria."

The cell phone store guy had neglected to mention that there were over 1,100 menus for us to "just follow." To complicate things, each menu we came to seemed to be slightly different depending on which other menu we were coming from, the overall context of the situation, and how we were holding our mouths at the time.

Of course, the phones had come with complete documentation. There was a "Quick Start Guide" which consisted of a diagram

What I've Learned So Far...

identifying a few important parts of the phone like "Send Key" and "Hinge," followed by a 12-page advertisement for purchasing music and videos from the cell phone company. The full "User's Manual" consisted of the same diagram followed by a couple of pages of information and a 64-page advertisement for purchasing music and videos from the cell phone company.

There was also a CD-ROM "Comprehensive Help Disc" that the label said I could run in my computer to get more detailed information. When I put it in, it started up automatically and presented us with a 27-minute advertisement for purchasing music and videos from the cell phone company.

The documentation may not have been very helpful, but it was pretty fun to read. It had apparently been written in Japanese then translated into English by somebody who had, at best, a vague grasp of either language. Or possibly by Yoda;

"If not working your phone is, press and hold the red button you must."

A week or so later our son dropped in for a visit. He found us still sitting dazed in the living room, muttering things like, "Phone not in 1x-EVDO coverage area – PPP session active," and repeatedly trying to test-call each other.

Part I: Bikes, Docks & Slush Nuggets

In less than ten minutes he had both phones making and receiving calls; he had our names displayed in banners on the little screens over languid pastoral scenery; he had our directory and speed dial settings organized; and he had my GPS feature enabled, so I had only to push a button to hear a pleasant feminine voice telling me, "Your destination, the bathroom, is four paces ahead... three... two... one... Turn Left Now! He even got rid of the ring tone that I had my phone stuck on, which was apparently a recording of a moose giving birth to a tractor.

I'm just hoping we can get him to come home for the holidays; by then I'll need to check my voice mail.

The Santa Clause

From the Law Offices of
Pimberton and Marlowe, PC

December 26, 2006

Mr. Kris Kringle
Chairman and CEO
St. Nicholas Enterprises, LLC
The North Pole

Dear Mr. Kringle,

As a senior partner here at Pimberton and Marlowe I'm writing to you as a follow-up to our pre-Christmas correspondence and our firm's subsequent research.

First though, let me thank you for your prompt and thoughtful advice regarding that personal issue we discussed last week. You were right, the keys to a silver 2007 335i Coupe under the tree for my wife did indeed make up for my regrettable lapse of judgment at the firm's Christmas party.

But down to business. Just as you suspected, our research team has found that there does exist a substantial loophole in your contract's current Naughty/Nice Determination Guidelines. To be specific, the exact language of Section 2, Subparagraph 3 is as follows:

2.3 Naughty/Nice Determinations shall be applied during one calendar year running from 12:00 AM on January 1 through 11:59 PM on December 31 of that same year.

And later, in Section 17, Subparagraph 9 the contract states:

17.9 Punishment for any of the above-described Naughty infractions shall be exacted on Christmas morning, December 25, of the calendar year during which said infractions were committed, specific punishment to be determined according to the following sentencing guidelines...

As you suspected, these two statements combine to form what we here at Pimberton and Marlowe like to call the "Santa Clause" (just a little seasonal lawyer humor there – ha, ha) which says in effect that all naughty behavior taking place during a calendar year is dealt with on December 25 of that year, while "new and actionable" naughty behavior only begins to accrue on January 1 of the following year. Thus the contract creates a sort of "free week" during which naughtiness cannot be punished.

So yes Kris, there is a "Santa Clause" (hee, hee, hee - oh my!).

Sorry.

As to your proposal suggesting how this situation might be rectified, every member of your legal team feels that your legal position on this idea would be tenuous at best. We admit that there is logic and even a certain appeal to the idea of dispatching teams of elves to selectively "repossess" Christmas gifts on the day after New Year, based on Naughty/Nice data collected during the week in question. And we even like your proposed name for the new holiday: "Looting Day."

However, we see several potential difficulties with this idea, not the least of which is the statutory matter of "Breaking and Entering." While we have in the past always been successful in defending you against B&E charges (141 times so far – it just doesn't seem possible, does it?), we have always done so on the basis that your activities could not be construed as burglary since you were leaving, not taking things.

Additionally, and as you are well aware, we are already on constitutional thin ice with that whole "He sees you when you're sleeping" issue. With that class-action Invasion of Privacy lawsuit pending, the idea of specifically adding a week of surveillance to your current activities would be ill-advised at best.

And so as your legal advisors, we must recommend that you pursue no immediate action regarding the "Santa Clause." Your overall Performance Agreement comes up for review in two years, and we feel that we may be able to contractually remedy the situation at that time. In other words, for now you should just take the week off and enjoy it.

I know I'm going to.

As always, we here at Pimberton and Marlowe are honored that you have selected our firm to represent your interests.

Sincerely,

Kevin Pimberton

Senior Partner

Help for the Shopmentally Challenged

The Holidays are here again, and throughout the land families are getting ready for the fun. The average mom is working day and night, addressing the cards, planning the merry-making, and doing everything in her power to make sure that this Christmas will be the best ever. The average child is erupting in a sustained explosion of anticipatory excitement, like a little bottle-rocket in matching mittens and stocking cap.

And the average husband is curled up somewhere in a fetal position, sucking his thumb and counting the minutes until the specter of Christmas shopping has passed.

Yes, this may come as a shock to many of my female readers, but men really aren't all that good at shopping. You see, women seem to find

Part I: Bikes, Docks & Slush Nuggets

an endless source of joy in spending nine or ten straight hours going from store to store in search of just the right shade of black pants. An experience like that would have just about any guy spending the next twenty years waking up in cold sweats and screaming for the mercy of a quick and painless check-out. In fact, there are now support groups available for the uniquely male victims of what has come to be known as Post-Traumatic Shopping Disorder.

Ladies, there are several reasons you should learn not to expect much from your man in the way of Christmas shopping. First, by your standards a man is as color-blind as a beagle. If you say, "I'd like a blue sweater," we will simply go out and buy you a sweater that is blue.

Now, you will probably be amazed to learn that a man cannot grasp the absurdity of doing that. And you should know that on Christmas morning when you patiently explain to us, "It's really nice, but I need robin's egg to go with that mocha skirt your sister gave me, and this is actually more of a periwinkle," as far as your man is concerned you might as well be speaking Swahili.

Second, our concept of how clothing should fit is very different from yours. To most men, if a Large is comfortable, it just stands to reason that an Extra-Large will be Extra-Comfortable. This

What I've Learned So Far...

is apparently not quite how women look at it. A woman's main priority when it comes clothing size is to have the smallest number printed on the tag while still being able to stuff her body into said clothing without either risking a complete loss of peripheral circulation or triggering a matter-antimatter implosion.

To further raise a guy's blood pressure and leave him sitting in the Mall fountain babbling dialogue from King Lear, it seems that the numbers describing a woman's clothing size vary depending on the store you happen to be in. This means that a "nine" in the Bulimia Boutique is not the same as a "nine" in Bertha's Palace for Plus-Size Goddesses.

Finally, the male of our species has an extremely short attention span where money is concerned. Women treat a purchase like a savings account, buying things on the premise that they can "always take it back." For this reason I believe that a woman keeps a sort of mental passbook of all her purchases, so she always has a pretty good idea of what she wants, what she has spent, and what she has in "return reserve."

For a guy, once a dollar is spent, he considers it spent. He buys whatever he thinks is cool, and expects it to stay bought. Don't tell him any different, and the odds are he will never know.

Part I: Bikes, Docks & Slush Nuggets

So ladies, try to be understanding when your husband cheerfully hands you a gift-wrapped Swiffer, a lime green pant suit, and a gross of AA batteries on Christmas morning. Just remind yourself that the poor guy is shopmentally challenged - and you can always take it back.

Another Medical Interlude

Not too long ago I treated my readers to the details of my colonoscopy, an often-feared medical procedure that turned out to be a bit of a technological miracle. Of course, after that little excursion to a place where (almost) no-one has gone before, it's also a bit of a miracle that I have any readers left.

Well, here we go again. Recently, inspired by a particularly poignant episode of *Family Guy*, I performed a self breast-exam. Ok, go ahead and do a quick gender check on the name of the author and the photo at the top of this column – I'll wait.

Back? Ok yes - I am, and as far as I know always have been, a man. What happened is that in this particular *Family Guy* the protagonist, Peter, found a lump in his breast and thought he was dying of breast cancer. Watching, I thought to myself, "Ha, ha, ha, wouldn't it be ironi... Hey, what the heck is this?"

As a quick (considering the use of the word "breast" in a Google search) visit to the Internet confirmed, guys can get breast cancer, even though it's rare.

Now when men are young, we all think that we look pretty darn good with our shirts off. At this point in our lives we call our breasts "pects," short for "pectoral muscles," and we believe that all the girls really dig them. Therefore, we tend to parade around a lot with our shirts off.

As we get older, most of us accumulate enough wisdom to realize we were generally wasting our time with the whole shirt-off thing. Of course, over those years our bodies also accumulate a fair number of pizzas, beers, Slim Jims and glazed donuts, because of which our cool "pects" grow to become the dreaded "man-boobs," or "moobs."

The point of all this is that no man is really crazy about having moobs, much less finding a lump in them. Nevertheless there it was, a lump about the size of an old-fashioned jelly bean. Not one of those frou-frou little Jelly Bellies, mind you, but a genuine *they-may-be-different-colors-but-they-all-taste-the-same-except-of-course-for-the-*

What I've Learned So Far...

black-ones-which-nobody-has-ever-actually-tasted-but-we-can-assume-that-they-are-nasty jelly bean. So I did the one thing that the average man does less often than he loans out his toothbrush – I called the doctor.

The doctor said he wasn't too worried about it, but he referred me to a surgeon who was also not too worried about it (why should they be worried – it wasn't their jelly bean), but he thought it should come out just to be on the safe side.

During the days leading up to my surgery, I couldn't help doing a little research. In 2005, 1,764 American men were diagnosed with breast cancer, and 375 of them died. That does count as relatively rare - in that same year, 41,116 women died out of the 186,467 who were diagnosed – the seventh most common cause of death for American women.

At last I found myself lying on a table with one arm over my head, locally anesthetized and getting a lumpectomy. I never had that sort of surgery before, since the overwhelming majority of my previous experience with hospitals has involved episodes of what health care professionals officially refer to as Done This Times - as in, "What has that knucklehead Done This Time?"

The surgery itself turned out to be amazingly quick, simple, and painless. And my jelly bean

Part I: Bikes, Docks & Slush Nuggets

turned out to be a "lipocyst," essentially an accumulation of pizza, beers, Slim Jims and glazed donuts that had turned into fat then decided to form that smooth little lump, just to keep things interesting. I was lucky.

1,764 men and 186,467 women were not so fortunate.

I have to say that for me the most uncomfortable thing about the whole experience was trying to convince the cute and somewhat puzzled young receptionist at the doctor's office that I was not teasing her, that I really did need an appointment because I had found a lump in my breast.

Apparently she had missed that episode of *Family Guy*.

Ok, So It's The End Of The World

Not too long ago the Sci Fi Channel produced a TV special, called "Countdown To Doomsday" in which experts consider ten really nasty ways human civilization might come to an end. Possibilities include invasion by aliens (I think they mean the kind that likes to abduct and conduct experiments on the residents of trailer parks in Alabama, rather than the housekeeping staff from the Red Roof Inn), getting into a cosmic fender-bender with an uninsured giant meteorite (our planet does not have airbags), or becoming slaves to a generation of ruthless futuristic killer robots (not including the one who is currently the Governator of California).

Despite the Sci Fi Channel's credentials as an unimpeachable scholarly institution, and even

Part I: Bikes, Docks & Slush Nuggets

though the possibilities they present are pretty darned scary, I think they've overlooked one of the most significant dangers facing our world today. I refer, of course, to Sudden Catastrophic Loss of Cellular, or SCLOC (pronounced, "SCLOC").

Ok, now granted that SCLOC might not seem as unpleasant as being pureed for lunch by a seven foot tall carnivorous avocado from Rigel 9, but appearances can be deceiving. Just picture the following nightmare scenario:

You're driving down the street, using your cell phone to make sure that your sister is current on all the critical details of your last dental check-up. Everything seems perfectly normal - birds are singing, traffic is flowing, and pedestrians are leaping to relative safety as you weave past, shouting, "Not lost – I said 'flossed!'"

At that moment, somewhere near Encino, California, a cellular technician is taking an unauthorized lunch break at his workstation. Distracted because he is also downloading the latest Dungeon Master Centerfold screen saver for his pc, he accidentally knocks his cup of gazpacho into the main control terminal, causing a cascading power failure that takes down the entire North American Cellular Grid.

Back in your car, your phone connection suddenly goes dead. Steering with your knees,

What I've Learned So Far...

you redial. Nothing. You check all your phone's indicators, looking for any way to explain the malfunction - the battery shows more than half-charged; your Dungeon Master Centerfold wallpaper looks ok; you paid the bill last Tuesday, and you're really sure the check should have cleared before the 15th.

You look up to see a motorist coming from the opposite direction, shaking his phone and banging it on the steering wheel. He sees you, swerves, and then plunges into a ravine, his car bursting into flames. As he disappears from view he shouts into his Bluetooth headset, "Can you hear me? Bill? Hello? HELLOOOOOOOOOooooooo?"

You try rebooting your phone, and your car veers off the road and into the crowded main hallway of a high school. Kids shrieking the names of friends into their own inert iPhones and frantically trying to retrieve the pictures they took at Caitlin's party last weekend flash past your windows. The assistant principal disappears beneath your onrushing car, typing his frantic last words into his Blackberry – a message that will, tragically, never be delivered.

Abandoning your vehicle in the lunch room under a pile of Salisbury steaks and tater tots, you stagger back out into the street, tenderly cradling your lifeless cell phone. Distant explosions and screams of, "You're breaking up! Hello?" assault your ears. At that moment you realize that the unthinkable has happened – the entire world around you is no longer "In Touch!"

Falling to your knees you look skyward, seeking some answer or shred of comfort in the heavens, overcome by the stark realization that your sister may not find out what the dentist said about your abscessed molar until you get home and call her on the land line. All hope is lost.

May Verizon help us all!

Where Can You Buy A Chew Toy For An iPod?

I got an iPod for Christmas. This proves that you can accomplish just about anything if you put your mind to it. And you're willing to whine a lot.

Now, up until this point in my life I didn't figure on ever having anything quite as - well, as extravagant as an iPod. Back in those dark Pre-iPod (PiP) days, I was ignorant of the fact that no normal adult could afford at any time to be caught as much as a hundred feet away from his copy of Houses of the Holy.

(If you have no idea what Houses of the Holy might be, the chances are you weren't born when Led Zeppelin recorded it. And if, like me, you came of age in the 1960s and were around to remember Houses of the Holy, the odds are pretty

Part I: Bikes, Docks & Slush Nuggets

good that you don't - 1960s and all. So in either case, I wouldn't worry about it.)

So anyway, now I'm an iBeliever. I have my 1,715 favorite songs loaded on my iPod, accessible at the push of a button - actually, three pushes, a few laps around the wheel with my thumb, another push or two, then the realization that I'm still not getting my brain liquefied by Houses of the Holy because I left the "ear buds" at home next to the coffee pot.

Getting an iPod is kind of like getting a pet. At first it's an iPuppy, all adorable and iPerfect. All you want to do is gaze at it, and cuddle it, and scratch it behind it's cute little USB port. But it's even better than a pet, because it never eats your wallet or iPiddles on your lap.

Since you love your little iPod, you just naturally want to buy it iPresents. Well, as luck would have it, an entire industry has grown up to help you satisfy this urge, and in a lot of stores these days you can find whole aisles full of nothing but iPod accessories.

You can spend $40 on a little canvas jacket with leather trim to protect it from getting scratched and, presumably, from catching the slightest iChill. You can spend anywhere from $50 to $800 on speaker systems with iPod docks built right in, so you can convert the most portable music system the world has ever seen into a living room-bound console stereo. You can pay $30 for a little kickstand that lets you prop your iPod up next to your 44-inch plasma television and watch *Gone With The Wind* on its 2.5" (diagonal) screen.

You can not, to the best of my knowledge, buy your iPod a squeaky toy or a neat little bed to sleep on - although I have heard a rumor that sometime in the second quarter of this year Apple is planning to release a new product that will give your little friend a place to rest, code-named iCot.

So here I am, the happy master of a bounding little iPod. The only problem I have is what to call the little rascal, which is actually something of an ongoing problem for me. All of the many animals that have come into my life were rescued, and came with a name, and I never felt really qualified to override fate in these matters. Unlike most men, I don't even have names for my body parts.

With this in mind (not the body parts thing, but the larger naming issue), I'm announcing the Name Mike's iPod contest. If you have a suggestion for me, just send it to nametheipod@learnedsofar.com, and I'll announce the winner in a future column.

Just for the record, I've already ruled out "iPoddie."

Sniffing Out the Myth of the "Weaker" Sex

My son and I recently went into a candle store to buy my wife a candle for a gift. On purpose. Just the two of us guys.

What could we have been thinking?

When I was a kid, there were two kinds of candles in my world. First, there was the tall, skinny kind that would sleep quietly all year long in that kind of flat little drawer in the dining room until Thanksgiving day, when they would get ritually melted onto the good lace tablecloth.

The other kind were much smaller and lived in a kitchen drawer with the screwdriver and the superglue until your birthday, when they would get ritually melted onto your birthday cake. In either case, the only real aromas involved with these candles came from the sulfur in the matches when you lit them and that burned-wick smell when you blew them out.

Now, just about every husband has been through the trial-by-nostril of accompanying his wife into a modern candle store. When the door opens you have to actually lean against the wall of fragrance that blasts out of the place. And if you know what's good for you, you crank up your best beatific smile for when she gives you that look of ecstasy and says, "Mmmmmm, doesn't this place just smell *scrumptious?*"

Your entire mission in the candle store is to follow her around with that smile frozen on your face while she shoves candles under your nose and says things like, "Oooh, this smells just like applesauce and garlic with just a hint of thyme!"

Ok, I'll admit that the candle in question really does smell just like applesauce and garlic with just a hint of thyme, and that is a part of my problem. You see, I happen to want all of the substances in my life that smell like food to be food. You can actually buy a candle that smells exactly like mashed potatoes, but I doubt that any amount of butter and salt would make it work out particularly well next to a chunk of meat loaf.

So as my son and I were staggering through the candle store, fighting for breath and watching wives subject their husbands to periodic bouts of Cranberry-Pecan-Mountain-Breeze asphyxiation, I began to wonder how the respective sniffers of men and women could be so different.

Think about it – in many respects, your average man has a pretty resilient sense of smell. He can casually plunge his nose into a shirt plucked from the laundry pile, then put that shirt on and wear it to work if the odor doesn't actually cause a seizure. He can happily chat and drink a beer after a game in a hockey locker room filled with his fellow "Masters" (old guys like me), as house flies swoon and fall dead in the airspace over the equipment bags.

A man will even generously share with his friends the most unique smells he encounters; "Hey Ted, give this a sniff – how long do you figure it's been dead?" And yet, his wife can chase them both into the garage with just a spritz of Artichoke-Gardenia-Cheesecake air freshener.

All I can figure is that women possesses a virtually superhuman level of olfactory toughness. They can easily survive for hours at a time in a closed space with a man and the entire range of creative fragrances he can produce, then stroll nonchalantly through the cosmetic department of a department store without supplemental oxygen.

And they were once called the "weaker sex!"

An iRose By Any Other Name

A couple of weeks ago I wrote about my new iPod, and in the process I invited readers to help me come up with a name for the cute little rascal. Well, I got a number of suggestions, including the idea of using an unpronounceable symbol, sort of like The Artist Formerly Known As Prince, Then That Stupid Symbol, And Now Known As Prince Again For The Benefit Of The Eleven People Who Still Give A Rip. And the winner is;

"iBall."

This name was first submitted by EB of Somewhere In North America, and independently a few days later by Dawn M. of Somewhere Else In North America. Runners-up include "iMike," iPathetic (which really would refer more to me than my iPod), and, in an apparent homage to either Bart Simpson or Rickey Ricardo, "iCarumba." The winners will each receive a trip, at their own expense, to anywhere they feel like going. And my undying gratitude.

In the same column, I also made a comment about naming inanimate objects like cars, boats, guitars, kitchen appliances, or body parts.

(Depending on our relationship with me, you can feel free to insert your own jokes regarding the inanimate nature of my body parts here.)

Done? All right then.

Anyway, my comment was that with a few exceptions, I don't do name things. Those exceptions are my gas grills, the late "Carl" and his successor, the magnificent "Enterprise." And now, of course, my new bosom companion, "iBall." This remark triggered a flood of concern from people who felt that I was missing an essential part of the human experience if I didn't go ahead and call my lawn mower "Kevin."

This got me wondering why we name things in the first place. Ok, I know why we name our kids and animals. We do it so we have a way to constantly demonstrate how completely parenthood has scrambled our brains. In my son's entire life I don't think I've ever said his name without first cycling through all my other relatives, every pet I've ever owned, and the starting lineup of the 1984 Detroit Tigers. At least the infield.

It does make sense that at some point in our evolutionary past we came up with the generic names we use for the things around us. It is a lot more efficient to say, "Please hand me that salad fork," than it is to gesture in the general direction of the salad fork and say, "Ngyuuuuhhh!" I know, because I've tried it both ways.

The question is why some folks feel obliged to go the extra mile and call the salad fork "Peetie."

A friend sent me this observation; "I believe we name things because without the manifestation of word as reality (i.e., the Greek "Logos"), there would be no reality as we perceive it."

I'm not real sure, but I think this means that if somebody, somewhere doesn't go ahead and call that salad fork "Peetie," the physical universe will cease to exist. This particular friend is really smart, so what she says is probably true. I'm just glad that there are people around who are willing to pick up the slack with little Peetie and all the other salad forks, and in so doing keep our cosmos clicking along.

I think Jean-Paul Sartre, the great French novelist and existentialist philosopher, described this idea best when he said, "Je ne sais quoi. Voulez vous couscous?" From what I can recall of

Part I: Bikes, Docks & Slush Nuggets

my high school French this translates as, "Beats the heck out of me. Do you want to have lunch?"

As for me, in the absence of the sort of intense emotional relationship that I have developed with my iPod and my gas grill, I'll just go on calling the objects around me "the car" or "those bricks" or "that handful of salted peanuts."

Just call me "Slacker."

A Couple of Old Rings

I have a ring that just turned thirty years old.
Thirty years.

I can remember being about seventeen and thinking that I was not real sure I even wanted to live for thirty years. I mean, think about it – thirty! How could a person that old have anything left to live for?

It's a simple gold ring, kind of medium-wide, with a pattern of leaves inscribed around it. Some of the detail in the leaves has worn away, ground down by thirty years of duty on a hand that held wrenches, and cameras, and cobbler's nails, and ski ropes, and power saws, and guitars, and maybe an occasional beer bottle. A hand that typed hundreds of thousands of words on a portable typewriter, and later on a computer keyboard.

A hand that knew the joy of holding the hand of a little boy who always seemed to find some comfort in its size and strength.

There's another ring around here that's just like mine, and just as old, only this one is a little bit smaller. The hand it's riding on is smaller too. It's a hand that still feels like it fits as perfectly into my hand as it did thirty years ago.

Thirty years ago an engraver scratched on the inside of each of these rings, "NJB to JMB, 7/19/75." Thirty years ago these inscriptions were a lot easier to read, with our young and hopeful eyes.

The nineteenth of July was exceptionally hot in 1975 – ninety-five degrees in the shade. We stood in a little stone chapel near the University of Michigan campus, where the only breath of air was stirred by a couple of box fans and fifty or so people waving their programs in front of their faces. We all ignored the perspiration dripping off my nose and spoke the few words that we had written for each other. The organist, suspended on the verge of heat exhaustion, started playing the recessional in the middle of the vows. We all stood and waited patiently for her to finish so we could carry on.

Then I put Nancy's ring on her finger and she did the same with mine.

Thirty years.

These rings saw warm summer days and frosty winter nights. They saw blue skies and gray skies. And, once, they saw a storm that came perilously close to putting an end to all of us.

They bathed in the unconditional love of three dogs and five cats. They watched us transform one house into a home, and then another one. They were washed with tears of pain, and tears of defeat, and tears of triumph.

They saw that little boy hold his first "sippy cup," and saw him score his first hat trick. They watched him tie his first necktie. They saw him getting his high school diploma wearing a red robe and a ridiculous flat hat. They saw him, tall and proud, packing his possessions and heading off to college. And they've really only seen the beginning.

Now that I think of it, the detail on the leaves surrounding our rings hasn't really been worn away. Those are just the spots where life, and love, and hardship, and happiness have polished them to a brilliant glow.

Thirty years. Please God, if it's not too much trouble, I'll take thirty more.

Part I: Bikes, Docks & Slush Nuggets

Lights! Camera! Bathrobe! Meet YouTube!

Did you know that there is a Web site where you can see a robot doing stunts on a skateboard, or Chad Vader (Darth's brother) using the dark side of The Force in his unfulfilling job as night manager of a grocery store?

There is – it's called YouTube.

On YouTube you can watch a girl getting shot across her back yard from a giant sling shot. You can watch $60,000 worth of iPods falling over like dominos and finishing by knocking an iBook off a pedestal. You can watch a seventh grade boy griping about his science teacher and making faces about his lab partner.

You can watch a guy who owns a guitar and whose mom cuts his hair, sitting on his bed playing the two guitar chords he knows and singing a really, *really* long original (mostly) song. You can watch an undiscovered Fellini or Bergman or Kurosawa unfold his artistic genius in unedited footage of a guy, whose mom cuts his hair, driving around a suburban neighborhood (in his mom's Volvo).

You can watch a dark, grainy, out-of-focus video of a high school girl in her bedroom, wearing a pair of boxer shorts and a tank top, dancing to the music of Gwen Stefani – 754,839 people had already enjoyed the version of this that I ran across.

You know, I find it a little bit surprising that a twenty-something man could believe that other people might want to watch him in a five minute film sitting at a messy table in a wife-beater and needing a shave, humming a White Stripes song and eating a bowl of corn flakes. I find it even more surprising that he is right - YouTube is one of the most active Web sites on the Internet.

Now I don't think this is entirely new behavior for our species. After all, one of the first things anybody does when they get their first camera is take a picture of themselves in a mirror, achieving deep philosophical insights that rank right up there with the realization that "dog" is "god" spelled backward.

Part I: Bikes, Docks & Slush Nuggets

In the past, though, very few people felt the need to send those mirror pictures to the New York Times.

When the Communication Age came along, featuring the Internet, everything changed. Social networking sites and blogs mean that suddenly our innermost thoughts can go out to the world in an instant, not wasting any time rattling around in our brains (where we might sort out whether or not they made any sense).

And now, with YouTube we can at last document for posterity the sights and sounds and raw emotions involved in opening and using a brand-new bottle of drain cleaner.

The really amazing thing is that YouTube is almost irresistible, kind of like watching a train wreck or a George W. Bush speech. You can find yourself strangely fascinated when people you've never met share, in authentic shaky-cam, their experience pulling down a dead maple tree with a pickup truck. Or when three completely self-absorbed young girls take you on a video tour of a MacDonald's ladies room.

Contrary to what you might have heard, the stuff on YouTube may be outrageously strange, and sometimes a little bit suggestive, but there isn't any really naughty stuff there. At least, I couldn't find any - no matter how hard I tried.

A Screwdriver Is More Than Just A Drink – Who Knew?

If there is one recurring theme in my column (and I can assure you there is at least one, since recurring themes can save a busy writer like me many hours of tedious work, like doing research or coming up with new ideas), it would be that I am not real good at fixing things.

Let's put this in perspective. I've often admitted that like most guys, I possess the Cool Tool Gene, that inborn and uniquely male attraction to anything that is metal, makes lots of noise, and has a power cord or a rechargeable battery. And like most guys, I've spent years collecting as many cool tools as I can afford. At this point I have a saw, two drills, and something that looks really interesting, called a "belt sander."

Now I know that a lot of guys use their tools to build stuff, or to fix stuff that is broken. I admire this. I do. I would love to know how to use that belt sander, or at least have some idea what a belt sander might be used for.

The bottom line is, if I need something built or fixed, even though I may have the very tools in my closet that would be perfect for the job, I am forced to grab my checkbook and call a guy with "Bob" stitched on the pocket of his coverall to come over and bail me out.

The instruction manuals that came in the boxes with the tools are no real help. Instead of any useful information - for instance, what kind of belts a person might want to sand – what you get is a series of vaguely Asian-looking silhouette people doing things like holding the tool while standing in a puddle of water and thus getting electrocuted, or jamming their silhouette fingers painfully into the business end of a band saw.

So the question is, where did Bob learn about using a band saw, beyond keeping his hands out of the blade? I would say that it is a fairly safe bet he did not pick it up in good old "Shop Class" at school. In fact, I'm pretty sure most Shop Classes don't even go so far as to cover the information in those instruction manuals – have you ever met a Shop teacher who had ten fingers?

It could be that Bob learned how to use tools from his father. This would explain a lot in my case, since my dad's concept of a "screwdriver" pretty much started and ended with vodka and orange juice.

I don't know though. My brother-in-law is a skilled electrician, and one of those guys who could single-handedly build a four-bedroom bungalow armed with nothing more than a hammer, a miter saw, and a six-pack, while his dad, rest his soul, was in way over his head if he had to change the bulb in a table lamp.

Maybe tool knowledge is one of those "genetic memory" things, like a salmon sensing which stream it's supposed to swim up, or a telemarketer sensing the exact instant your first bite of pork chop is on the fork. Yes, gazing back through the long evolution of our species, I can just see Oog in his cave teaching little Oog, Junior how to use a small rock to bash a bigger rock into the shape of a water softener.

Then there would be my ancestor, Mikk, coming to the cave door with his checkrock in hand because the genetic memories would already have passed him by. He would have a cool flint axe and an obsidian belt sander sitting in the garage, but no idea how he might use them to add on that rumpus room for Mrs. Mikk.

And so my ancestor would have called for someone who could help. Someone who, of course, would have "Bob" stitched on the pocket of his saber tooth tiger skin.

Where Have All The Heroes Gone?

When we first moved to our lake here in Michigan, there was a yearly event called Winterfest. Aside from Christmas, this was hands-down the best part of the long, gray, slush-up-your-pant-leg, toe-numbing, car-door-rotting, sniffles-producing chunk of our year that Winterfest is named after.

The first official ritual of Winterfest came in early January when everybody around the lake would dispose of their Christmas trees by simply dragging them out onto the ice and leaving them there. Before long, friendly oversized gremlins wearing parkas and sturdy boots would come along and take them away. These were members of the local Kiwanis Club, who would use our trees, gallons of green dye, snow shovels, ice augers, and a little imagination to design and build an Ice Golf course right out there on the frozen lake.

Ice Golf was played with a tennis ball and one club, usually a crappy old seven iron - although a few big hitters were willing to sacrifice putting accuracy to gain the backspin and subtle touch around the greens they could get from the more lofted crappy old nine.

As soon as the ice was more than a couple of feet thick, while the Kiwanians were still painting greens and sculpting snow traps around piles of pine needles, people would take their cars and trucks out to join the snowmobiles, charging around the lake in joyful defiance of nature, common sense, and insurance statistics. By the peak weekend of Winterfest, there would be helicopters, and monster trucks, and ice-diving exhibitions, and, of course, golf tournaments.

None of this happens any more. The standard explanation is that the winters lately haven't been nearly as cold as they used to be, so we're no longer sure to get enough ice. This is true, but there is another ingredient that also seems to have come into short supply:

The heroes who used to make it happen.

Last weekend our community held a tribute to a neighbor who is in the final stages of his battle with cancer. As our neighbor, we've mostly known

What I've Learned So Far...

Duane for the past few years as the big, smiling, gentle, bald grizzly bear, striding around the edge of the lake to get the exercise his doctor prescribed after his bypass surgery. Or we knew him as the smiling grizzly bear who would show up at the library on the fourth of July every year to recite In Flanders Fields and sing the National Anthem in his beautiful baritone.

At his tribute, we were reminded that Duane served in the 1st Infantry Division (the Big Red One) during World War II and fought in the Battle of the Bulge. We were reminded that he served as a decorated police detective in Ann Arbor. We were reminded that he served as president of the School Board who built the high school that has educated the kids in our community (including my son) for more than fifty years. We were reminded that he served on the state governing board of the Kiwanis Club.

We were reminded that he served in his church choirs, barber shop quartets, and in any other singing group that was in need of the joyful noise he loved to produce. We were reminded that he has served as loving patriarch to a family that has successfully modeled itself on his example of quiet strength and profound sense of duty.

We were also reminded that he was one of those gremlins in parkas and sturdy boots who used to drag our discarded Christmas trees around the lake.

You see, along with all of the truly monumental things Duane accomplished in his life, he and a lot of other heroes like him were willing to empty their enormous reservoirs of energy into an event that really served no purpose other than adding a marvelous dash of excitement and happiness to the lives of his family, his friends and his neighbors.

What a wonderful purpose.

Unfortunately, many of us are now too busy making deals, or investing our money, or planning vacations, or making sure we don't miss a single episode of The Sopranos to organize events like Winterfest. So we've left this kind of work to the people like Duane, who had nothing better to do with their lives than survive the Great Depression, and win World War II, and pretty much build the modern world we inhabit.

As time goes by, all of these folks are inevitably moving on to the Next Great Adventure, leaving behind them a void that's not readily being filled by those of us on whose behalf they accomplished all those things.

Kind of makes you think, doesn't it?

And The Award Goes To...

Well, the Academy Awards are upon us once again. By the time this goes to press we will all be standing around the water cooler and expressing our shocked outrage about the no-talent pretty boy who stole the Oscar for The Best Use Of Optical Flow-Based Image Manipulation. Set the TiVo – I don't want to miss a minute!

We are, in fact, TiVo-ing our way toward the climax of The Season Of Eye-Watering Award Shows. This is that magic time of year when we get to watch, transfixed, as every possible subdivision of the entertainment industry gathers together to honor their members who in the past year have accumulated the most headlines without actually being indicted.

We've already been through the Golden Globe Awards, which is a sort of dress rehearsal for the

Part I: Bikes, Docks & Slush Nuggets

Academy Awards. The Golden Globe Awards are presented by the Hollywood Foreign Press Association, so the winners get to brag about their international appeal, while all the fans of the losers get to say, "Whut do them-there 'feriners know about art anyhow?"

Then come the Grammies, in which a parade of strangely-clad musicians troop up to the microphone to give all the credit for their accomplishments to God, the sycophants in their entourage, and the miracles of pharmaceutical chemistry. I have heard that the Grammy committee plans to introduce a lifetime achievement award for the Rap or Hip-Hop artist who has survived the most drive-by shootings.

This will dovetail perfectly with the honorary awards they've been giving out for all the ones who didn't.

The Country Music Awards are a nice contrast to the Grammies. These performers tend to be a lot more down-to-earth and, by and large, more deeply indebted for their artistic success to Jesus and Jack Daniels.

Of course there are the lesser-known shows. My favorite of these is Film Independent's Spirit Awards, honoring the year's finest independent films. Independent films are officially defined as, "Films with jack-squat for promotion budgets, so pretty much nobody will ever hear of them." Watching the Spirit Awards, you can learn about incredibly good work by innovative directors, writers and actors. Of course, you will probably never see any of this incredible work in a theater unless you live in New York, San Francisco, Sundance, or Cannes.

The best thing about any award show is the Red Carpet. This is the part where all the famous people walk into the venue past interviewers, photographers and adoring masses, and you get to see what the women are wearing. Ok, I know that sounds sexist, but that's just the way it is. A male celebrity's idea of daring attire is wearing blue jeans with a tuxedo, and Billy Bob Thornton burned that one out years ago.

The women, on the other hand, are always finding new and more interesting ways for their outfits to defy gravity and the censors. Every time a limo door swings open, we are teased with the tantalizing possibility that a wisp of silk will slip or a sequin will pop off, and we may get a momentary glimpse of a bit of anatomy that we could easily see our fill of, just by coughing up $8.50 for a ticket and another $12.00 for a diet Coke and a bucket of buttered popcorn.

I've always found all of this really entertaining to watch – purely, you understand, from the point-of-view of the theoretical physics involved.

Part I: Bikes, Docks & Slush Nuggets

I have recently become disillusioned, however, by the discovery that these women are not really tempting fate to the extent I had always imagined. It seems that there are clothing designers who specialize in creating these outfits to look daring, while employing the latest technological advances in polymer fabrics and two-sided carpet tape to maintain a family rating for the entire Red Carpet viewing experience.

There is a type of undergarment, called Spanx, that can hide beneath a whisper, and still squeeze two dress sizes off an actress who may have got a little too involved with a tub of buttered popcorn at her movie's premiere. There are even makeup artists who use an airbrush to add suntans, eliminate wrinkles, and even (I know this is absolutely true, because I read it on the Internet) add the appearance of toned muscles to all those areas that are not obscured by whispers and Spanx.

Oh well. I guess if I wanted reality, along with the genuine possibility of wardrobe malfunction, I should just stick with the halftime shows at the Superbowl.

A Pilgrimage To Paradise
Part 1 – We Always Drive Straight Through

Dad squints into the hot morning sun and crushes a new set of indentations into the steering wheel with a grip that only twenty-three solid hours of expressway driving and gas station coffee can produce. Mom snores next to him, drooling into a pillow propped against the passenger-side window. Todd Junior and Little Suzie are sprawled in the back seat, serenely drifting along in their childish dreams amid a haze of French fry and Twizzler fumes. Bernie The Schnauzer is seated between them trying to inconspicuously polish off the Super Jumbo bag of beef jerky propped between Todd Junior's legs.

The car rounds a long curve on the highway and passes a 1987 Cadillac, apparently being driven by a fedora hat and permanently signaling a right turn.

And then it happens. The Sign heaves into view, that warm green rectangle resplendent with glorious white letters shouting out the message that Dad has been anticipating throughout the past few hours of his caffeine-induced hallucinations:

"Pompano Beach – This Exit."

As he guides the car down the exit ramp, and after three tries at clearing his throat, he croaks, "We're here! Next stop, a whole week at Grandma and Grandpa's place!"

Mom snorts her way out of a dream involving a remote desert island, a bottle of champagne, a harem outfit, some light bondage, and Johnny Depp. Bernie The Schnauzer rockets into the front seat wearing the jerky bag on his head like a hood. And, as a matter of pure subliminal reflex, Todd Junior slugs Little Suzie on the arm.

Minutes later The Family pulls into the parking lot of Grandma and Grandpa's home for the winter, the Golden Palmetto Bug Motor Lodge.

Mom, Bernie The Schnauzer, and the kids bound out of the car and toward Grandma and Grandpa's room as Dad rolls out from under the steering wheel and onto all fours on the pavement, unable to straighten his legs. A gray-haired man wearing a canary yellow polyester aloha shirt, lime green polyester shorts, knee socks and sandals pauses next to Dad as he struggles to his feet and says, "Are you the plumber? Been waiting for you all day, boy. Them pipes ain't going to fix themselves, you know."

Given their eleven years of seniority at the Golden Palmetto Bug, Grandma and Grandpa's room is in a prime poolside location. Dad, Mom, Bernie and the kids have been assigned to a "Short Term Guest Room" a little further back in the rear of the old building, with a scenic view across the dumpster to Slick Al's Liquor Shack and the Pompano Porno Emporium.

By the time Dad has hauled the fifth load of luggage up to the room, the kids are in the pool, squealing with joy and pelting each other with the bits of waterlogged detritus they've found floating in the sparkling brown water. Mom is in a lawn chair showing Grandma the latest pictures of Stan and Stacy's new baby girl. It's eighty-five degrees in the shade and Grandpa, wearing a flannel shirt and corduroys, has gone in to get a sweater. Bernie the Schnauzer is over by the Coke machine, cornered by a cockroach the size of a cougar.

And so begins The Family's escape from the frozen north, their trek to spend a little time with Grandma and Grandpa in Florida.

A Pilgrimage To Paradise
Part 2 – The Fort Lauderdale Old Country Buffet

Todd Junior is lying on his belly on the roof of the cabana in the late morning sun with a water balloon in each hand, snickering and waiting for Little Suzie to come around the corner. Little Suzie is in the bathroom making up names for each of the 173 lizards who live in the toilet, and keeping an eye on the time. She wants to make certain that Todd Junior gets enough sun waiting for her out there on the roof of the cabana to actually go right past sunburned and straight to extra-crispy.

Mom is sitting in the shade by the pool with Grandma, sipping iced tea and chatting about Great Aunt Ellen's gall bladder. Dad is around the corner at the Pompano Porno Emporium trying to buy a copy of the New York Times, reasoning that, "After all, it is a bookstore – sort of." Grandpa, wearing a sweater, a ski jacket and a stocking cap, is rummaging around for his bottle of brandy and his earmuffs.

Bernie the Schnauzer, who had dozed off in a patch of sunlight, is being carried across the parking lot and toward the dumpster by two optimistic earwigs.

It's day three in The Family's stay at the Golden Palmetto Bug Motor Lodge in Pompano Beach, Florida. The highlight of the trip so far has been yesterday's gala Early Bird Special at Big Norma's Winn-Dixie View Café. Today, the focus of the fun will be on the traditional visit to the Senior Savings Hour at the Fort Lauderdale Old Country Buffet.

Grandma and Grandpa function on a carefully designed and maintained meal schedule. Grandma keeps a large message board in the kitchen, listing every discount at all of their favorite restaurants, organized by day of the week. For each entry she has a primary and at least one backup option listed - she doesn't want a repeat of the disastrous 1987 power failure fiasco at Ingrid's No-Need-To-Chew-It Smorgasbord.

Dad has given up his quest for the New York Times and returns from the Pompano Porno

Palace with the pupils of his eyes permanently dilated. Little Suzie's egg timer goes off, indicating that Todd Junior is roasted to perfection, so she lobs her own water balloon at him from the balcony overlooking the cabana. Mom and Grandma switch topics to Great Uncle Charlie's colonoscopy. Grandpa has found his earmuffs and his brandy, and has achieved a happy sort of thermal equilibrium.

Bernie the Schnauzer was startled awake and escaped when one of the earwigs tripped over a Toyota SUV, and is now in the grass behind the pool happily rolling in a nest of fire ants.

Just after lunch, they pack Bernie the Schnauzer in Calamine lotion, and everyone else into Grandpa's Buick, and they all head out toward the Old Country Buffet for dinner. On the way to Fort Lauderdale they take time to pass back and forth over the Intercoastal Waterway so that Grandpa can point out every wastefully lavish home or boat, along with his cost estimate. Then everybody takes turns speculating on how anyone could come up with that much money.

They reach the restaurant at exactly 4:00 PM, along with 1,400 other senior citizens. Todd Junior tries to convince Dad that a dinner plate full of pudding actually does constitute a balanced diet, since it incorporates every food group except broccoli. Mom, Grandma and Little Suzie each make a salad and find a table. Grandpa bumps his forehead on the sneeze shield and drops a mitten in the creamed corn.

On the way home, Todd Junior's sunburn starts to blister, providing Little Suzie with her carefully planned Anti-Todd Junior deterrent weapon system. Dad falls asleep in an Old Country Prime Rib coma. Mom and Grandma explore the topic of Aunt Meg and Uncle Bob's twins and their recent adventure with scabies.

Grandpa heads back to Pompano on the expressway this time, giving up the possibility of repeating Intercoastal Housing Critique in the interest of getting back to the Golden Palmetto Bug by their normal 7:30 PM bed time.

It's the end of another perfect day.

A Pilgrimage To Paradise
Part 3 – A Scientific Interlude With A Two-Headed Cow

Todd Junior's heartfelt request drifts on the clear Florida morning breeze like the sweet sound of a Chihuahua giving birth to a litter of St. Bernard puppies;

"I WANNA SEE MICKEY AND GOOFY!"

Dad rubs his eyes and says, "Look son, we've gone over this already. We've been to Disney World three times a year for the past nine years. We have the theme songs from every ride memorized. We're on a first name basis with all the ride attendants. I figure that we've spent around three grand each time we've gone there, which means that at this point Disney has something like $81,000 of my money. This time we're going to try something a little different."

Mom smiles at Todd Junior and says, "Besides, Key West will be fun! There are lots of gift shops!"

"Will there be rides?" sobs Todd Junior.

"No, but there are some of the best transvestite bars in North America," chirps Little Suzie, looking up from the copy of The Modern Queen's Guide To The Florida Keys that Mom mistakenly bought along with her Frommer's.

"I'll get everybody a new T-shirt!" says Mom, snatching the book out of Little Suzie's hands and tossing it into the pool.

And so The Family waves goodbye to Grandma and Grandpa, leaves the friendly confines of the Golden Palmetto Bug Motor Lodge in Pompano Beach and heads south. "Key West, here we come! Just 198 miles to go!" sings Mom.

Seven hours, a tank of gas, eleven drive-through's, and fifteen potty stops later, they pull into Key West. "That drive wasn't so bad," says Mom through clenched teeth.

"We're going to abandon the car here and fly home," says Dad.

Part I: Bikes, Docks & Slush Nuggets

"Look!" cries Little Suzie, "It's the Café La-Te-Da, home of the All Star She-Male Review..."

"I have to go poop," grunts Todd Junior.

Before long, The Family is walking happily down Duval street. Todd Junior, sporting a brand new "I'm With Stupid" t-shirt is trying to convince Little Suzie to walk next to him.

Little Suzie gives the rest of her melting chocolate ice cream cone to Todd Junior to supplement the interesting allegedly-edible abstract artwork already in progress on the front of his shirt.

Dad is wearing his new wrap-around sunglasses, trying not to get caught staring at the two young women wearing rollerblades and thong bathing suits on the sidewalk ahead of them.

Bernie the Schnauzer is temporarily forgotten, still tied to the streetlamp outside the gift shop where Dad purchased his sunglasses and four of the always-hilarious Invisible Dog On A Leash novelties.

And then Mom spots it – the fabled Ripley's Believe It Or Not Museum! Where else can you see, under one roof, a car made from ten thousand dimes, a two-headed calf, a vampire killing kit, a fake mermaid, and an autographed pair of Madonna's underpants?

And so, as the sun sets on Key West, the home of Ernest Hemingway's six-toed cats and the southernmost point in the Continental United States, we leave The Family, reaching the pinnacle of their vacation in a rigorous celebration of culture and the true spirit of scientific inquiry.

Just for the record, Key West is one of my favorite places on this planet. If you have never been there, you are living a sadly deprived life. Try to get there between mid-October and mid-May when the Stone Crab Claws are in season.

Part I: Bikes, Docks & Slush Nuggets

Hey, It Will Always Grow Back

I got a haircut this week.

Now to a lot of people this may not seem like a life-altering event but, as a child of the 1950s and 1960s, haircuts have always occupied a very special place in my personal universe. Gimme a head with hair, long beautiful hair...

When I was little, my dad took me with him to see Joe the Barber. Other than a few years off for World War II and a fair amount of job-related moving around the country, he had been going to Joe for haircuts since he was in high school. And for all those years Joe had been giving him exactly the same haircut, a tonsorial classic known as a "flat-top."

My younger brother had hair that behaved exactly like our dad's. With a few deft swipes of the electric clippers Joe the Barber could easily

What I've Learned So Far...

square off the top of his head so perfectly that my parents could stand him next to a chair, put a lamp on him and use him as an end table.

My hair was, unfortunately, not quite so cooperative. The closest I could get to a flat-top was a thing called a "Princeton," in which Joe would shave most of my head to a blonde stubble, leaving a little sheaf right at the front that he would paste into a vertical salute with an intensely sweet-smelling waxy grease called "Butch Wax."

As I got a little older I began to ask Joe the Barber to attempt some variations on the theme. He would always listen carefully as I described the cool way Rick Nelson's hair fell across his forehead, nodding thoughtfully and saying, "Sure thing," or "You betcha!"

Then he would shave most of my head to a blonde stubble, leaving a little sheaf right at the front that he would paste into a vertical salute with "Butch Wax." If I complained that this is not how Rick Nelson's hair looked, he would nod thoughtfully and say, "Well it's how he would look if he had a "Princeton."

By the time I was in high school, the length of a person's hair was becoming a symbol of social defiance, and I wanted more than anything to join The Movement. This led to the fateful day when the Assistant Principal glared at me across his desk

Part I: Bikes, Docks & Slush Nuggets

and handed me a dollar to go across the street to get a trim because I had hair touching the top of my ears.

Then came college, and I said goodbye to barber shops for a few years. The closest I ever came to a haircut in those days were those occasions when a girl friend would want to fool around with my shaggy locks and get rid of something called "split ends." As long as I had a supply of beer available and she didn't paste any of my hair straight up with 'Butch Wax," I was pretty much indifferent to the whole process.

For most of the years since those rebellious undergrad days, I've been forced by the norms of society to pay at least some attention to personal grooming. And this has forced me back into barber shops.

In the old Joe the Barber time, a barber shop was a distinctively "man" place. On a table in the corner sat a pile of assorted newspapers and Sports Illustrated magazines dating back a minimum of five years, along with a stack of Zane Gray novels. The aromas of shaving cream, Witch Hazel, and, of course, "Butch Wax" hung thick in the air. A radio on a shelf over the mirror was somehow, at least in my memory, always broadcasting a baseball game. The conversation among the men in the shop was always about sports, cars, lawn care, or politics.

What I've Learned So Far...

Women were not really welcome in barber shops. They went to a distinctly woman sort of place called a "beauty parlor" where there were magazines like The Ladies Home Journal and rows of beehive-shaped hair dryers. The smell was hair spray and ammonia, and the radio played soft music that would not interfere with the conversation about the shocking dress Angie wore to the potluck at church.

Those days are, by and large, gone. Not only do women now go into barber shops, they are often the barbers. And many men patronize what has become a "hair shoppe" rather than the old "beauty parlor," where they co-exist with women getting their hair curled and the color touched up. In fact, a lot of them get their own hair curled and the color touched up.

I'm not sure I would really want to go back to the old days. My haircuts arguably look a lot better now than they did when I was a kid. But as bad as they were, they always grew out.

Plus, I kind of miss the smell of "Butch Wax."

Part I: Bikes, Docks & Slush Nuggets

Watching The Real Deal

Yesterday my friend Scott asked me, "Did you see *American Idol* the other night? Man, I thought for sure Traci was going to make it, but they got rid of her and kept that moron Todd. And then that giant squid got hold of Miranda and Kevin, and he ripped out and ate their still-beating hearts, so now it looks like Todd, or even Clarissa, could win it all..."

Ok, I'll admit that I have never actually seen American Idol, so my recollection of everything Scott said after "Have you seen..." is kind of fuzzy. I could very well be wrong about the whole giant squid thing.

Anyway, let's put this into perspective. Scott is a guy who thinks that watching a stock ticker is nail-biting entertainment. The articles in the *Wall*

What I've Learned So Far...

Street Journal are sometimes just a little bit too playful for his taste. He watches CSPAN.

To put it plainly, most of the time Scott is an intelligent, serious individual.

And yet here he is, caught up in the human drama of a group of young amateur entertainers who try, week after week, to tailor their performances to please three judges - a bass guitar player; a slightly past-her-best-days singer; and an Englishmen who is qualified to judge the performances of young amateur entertainers because he was once involved in the *Mighty Morphin' Power Rangers* CD, and because he might just be the nastiest human being who ever walked the planet.

And in making that judgment, I have not forgotten about Caligula, Jack The Ripper, Vlad The Impaler, Carl Rove, and Dick Cheney.

Scott is not alone in his obsession with *American Idol*. Every week, millions of people watch the show so that they can vote against whatever Simon Cowell says. And millions more faithfully watch the endless stream of other "Reality Shows" that have come to dominate the pages of *TV Guide*.

The first Reality Show I can remember seeing was *Real World*, in which young, physically attractive contestants live together and continuously whine at each other, or about each other, until someone snaps and gets voted out of the house.

Then *Road Rules* came along, a show in which they did all these things while riding around in a Winnebago and entering greased pig contests.

Ok, I am aware that *Cops* - the show that proved to the world that you should never wear a stained tank top and sagging jeans if you intend to get really dunk, hit your wife with a frozen chicken pot pie, then have a chat with a police officer - was around for years before *Real World*. I choose not to define *Cops* as a typical Reality Show because instead of getting voted off, you get thrown down, handcuffed, and crammed into the back seat of a police cruiser.

Different kind of reality.

I think the Reality Show turning point was *Survivor*, which pits photogenic young adventurers and investment bankers against the brutal forces of nature. *Survivor* episodes have been filmed in remote locations all over the world, where the contestants' only tenuous links to civilization and survival itself are the crew trailer and the satellite uplink.

Over the past few years Reality Shows have proliferated like empty police cruisers in the parking lot at a Dunkin Donuts grand opening.

What I've Learned So Far...

We now have *Dancing With The Stars*, *America's Next Top Model*, *Blind Date*, *Beauty And The Geek*, *Fear Factor,* and countless other tests of human talent, endurance, and willingness to eat live earthworms.

We even have *The Search For The Next Doll*, in which athletic (ahem) young women in skimpy costumes compete for the chance to join Nicole, Ashley, Kimberly, Melody, Jessica and Carmit, to become a household name as a member of the world-famous Pussycat Dolls.

Ok, if you ever saw or heard of the Pussycat Dolls before this show – or, for that matter, before this column – please send me an email. I'd like to know what else you've been watching.

So what could be next on the Reality Show horizon? How do you top a bunch of pretty girls in string bikinis and hunky guys in board shorts falling off a crane and into the East river? Well, I'm thinking that a show featuring some sort of actual reality might be interesting. The kind of "reality" you and I experience.

Maybe something like:

America's Visa Card:

The Minimum Amount Due.

Not Really Suitable

Not too long ago I had to wear a suit. Honest, a jacket, a tie and everything. And socks!

The occasion was my nephew's wedding, and my wife convinced me that the Bermuda shorts, golf shirt and dress flip flops that I had laid out for the occasion would fail to demonstrate the proper respect for the occasion. Even though they were my good shorts. I was worried that if I went to the wedding wearing a suit, my nephew might not recognize me. And I was right; he thought I was a Jehovah's Witness.

There was a time, years ago, when I wore a suit to work every day. I did this on the advice of a guy named John T. Molloy, who told me to do it in his book, Dress For Success. Mr. Molloy made the point that to be taken seriously in the business world a young man had to dress in conservative,

What I've Learned So Far...

businesslike attire; like an FBI agent, only with better shoes.

His advice, thankfully, did not extend to dressing like long-time FBI director J. Edgar Hoover, who liked to dress like Lauren Bacall.

All of this took place during the 1980s, a golden time when we as a society decided to shake off all that messy altruism and free spirit from the '60s and '70s, and return to the core values of unbridled greed and corruption that shaped America in the first half of the twentieth century. Boy, did I ever want to get aboard that train!

Before I was introduced to the idea of using a power necktie to subjugate the proletariat and get a window office, my idea of getting dressed up was to put on relatively clean jeans and a tank top without too many holes in it. My hair was generally shoulder length, and every winter I would grow a beard that made me look like a scrawny Grizzly Adams.

For a short time in the mid '70s I did own what was called a "disco" suit, consisting of powder blue polyester pants, shirt and jacket, with two-tone platform shoes and matching belt. This is not something that I am proud of, but it is a sad tale that must be told. Astonishingly, my wife did not save any photographs of me in that outfit.

Like a lot of guys in my generation, my

antisocial dressing preferences probably date back to rebellion against a well-meaning mother who thought of her kids as dress-up dolls. One of my earliest memories is walking into a restaurant with my family, my brother and I dressed in matching black and red pedal-pusher pants and "cute little tops," with white socks and sandals.

Yes, it is possible for a five-year-old to both have fashion sense and to be suicidal.

My Dress For Success transition from hippy to predatory businessman had to be a little bit shocking for my wife. Even though she had been on hand, and even complicit in, the "disco outfit incident," she always seemed for some reason to be comfortable with a husband who looked like he came straight from the mud at Woodstock.

And yet through those years when she was picking up my dress shirts at dry cleaners and gently reminding me that the black socks would probably look better with the navy blue suit than the green argyle ones, she never complained.

Well, decades have passed, and I've abandoned the idea of putting on that Brooks Brothers battle gear so that I could become a captain of industry. Other than when she cleans me up for the occasional wedding or funeral, my wife has her happy vagrant husband back. And she does not complain. Go figure.

A Night In The Chest Pain Unit

Beep, beep, beep.

You wake up from a light, fitful sleep at 3 AM to the sounds of a heart monitor beeping and the semi-hushed voices of two nurses outside your room discussing household indiscretions of their husbands and kids. The I.V. stuck in the back of your hand keeps you from rolling onto your side to get comfortable. Your hospital gown is wadded and twisted around your various body parts in strange and awful ways.

And then it gets worse. You hear a weird change in the sounds coming from that heart monitor – your heart monitor - and you try not to imagine what could be going wrong inside your chest to make those changes.

But the voices of the nurses who are keeping track of your monitor don't even break stride,

Part I: Bikes, Docks & Slush Nuggets

and after a while you decide that what you heard was all in your imagination. Besides, you're so exhausted that at that point you no longer care, and so you doze back into that light, fitful sleep.

Beep, beep, beep.

Last week I went through a night just like that when, after carrying a few (104) lawn chairs up a flight of stairs, I felt a radiating pain in my left arm. With a family history like mine (I lost my father to heart disease when he was nearly ten years younger than I am now), this is something to take seriously.

When I walked into the hospital emergency room and told the triage clerk that I was experiencing symptoms of a heart attack, accompanied by a health insurance card, I got a fair amount of attention. I was ushered into a small room where a woman asked me a lot of questions, while a man stuck that I.V. needle in my hand, pasted a bunch of stickers on various parts of my body, and hooked electrodes to them.

Beep, beep, beep.

It seems that when the emergency room staff thinks you might be having a heart attack, stickers become their main priority. Every time they moved me from one room to another, someone would slap a few more stickers on me and attach more wires to them. By the time I was getting

What I've Learned So Far...

my fourth set, I asked my current sticker-sticker-oner why she couldn't just use the ones that were already there.

This was apparently the funniest thing she had heard in a while, because when she recovered from her helpless laughter and left the room, I could hear her in the hall repeating my question to, presumably, a breathlessly howling gang of other sticker-sticker-oners.

Beep, beep, beep.

At about midnight they checked me into a room in the Chest Pain Unit, where I received ten more stickers and a turkey sandwich. They also hooked a portable heart monitor transmitter thingy to my stickers, so the nurses could keep an eye on my vital signs if I should happen to get out of bed and wander down to the bathroom. I spent a fair part of the next few hours wondering what effect each of the various possible bathroom activities might have on the displays the nurses would see on their monitor screens out there at the nursing station.

Beep, beep, beep.

When nature overcame heart monitor modesty and I finally did wander down to the bathroom, there was a sign on the wall over the toilet that said, "No Smoking In The Chest Pain Unit." As a long-ago ex-smoker – which is the most sanctimonious kind of ex-smoker – it seemed a little crazy that you would have to tell people that. Then it occurred to me that smoking probably had a lot to do with at least some of my fellow chest pain unit patients being there in the first place.

Beep, beep, beep.

In the morning a pretty young blonde woman came around with a wheelchair to collect me. There are very few things I can think of that are harder on a man's self-esteem than wearing a hospital gown and something like fifty stickers, being pushed around in a wheelchair by a pretty young blonde woman.

She had come to take me for my "stress echo cardiogram," a test which involved the pretty young blonde woman putting more stickers and wires on my chest, then making me walk as fast as I could on a treadmill. Once the pretty young blonde woman and her treadmill had me wheezing like a steam engine, her partner (a pretty young brunette woman) made me lie down and hold my breath while she poked around my chest with a metal probe. Ok, this is one thing I can think of that is harder on a man's self-esteem than the wheelchair and hospital gown deal.

Beep, beep, beep.

Back in my room a few hours later, my nurse told me that the tests came out all right, and that I could go home and follow up with my own doctor. Then she disconnected my IV, harvested all my stickers, gave me my clothes, and wished me good luck.

To that nurse, and the pretty young women, and all the sticker-sticker-oners and other doctors and nurses who helped me through that frightening, uncomfortable, sometimes humiliating night I say, "Thank you." From the bottom of my heart.

Taking Inventory On Father's Day

This past Sunday was Father's Day. For me this was extra-special, since my birthday always falls within a couple days of Father's Day, which puts me in a league with people born on December 24 and people who get themselves locked overnight in bakeries. We all get a lot of a good thing, and we get it all at once.

So I'm thoroughly enjoying the "Guinness" and "Corona" boxer shorts that my wife gave me, and that cool "The Chef Is An Idiot" barbecue apron I got from my son. The cats chipped in and bought me a new can opener.

Life doesn't get any better than this.

Now television ads would imply that a guy might be disappointed with that kind of haul. They suggest that every dad should wake up on father's day to find that little BMW Z4 convertible they've had their eye on sitting in the driveway with a bow on it – as if Mom and the kids cracked open the Pocket Change Jar and found 168,000 quarters in it.

Well, you can count me right out of that scenario. For one thing, if you have cool things like BMWs you are, in turn, expected to be cool. You can't just drive around in a Z4 wearing a torn Barefoot Company t-shirt, sun-faded board shorts and flip-flops. And I'm not changing my wardrobe for any car!

But I think the bigger issue here is managing expectations. When you're a kid, you approach all gift-receiving holidays with a sense of unbridled avarice. You set your sights on getting that Batman outfit (complete with cowl, gauntlets and tool belt with a real working compass built in), and nothing will deter you. You even believe with all your heart that the outfit will actually turn you into Batman, so you can suit up and take retribution on that bigger kid who pushed you down and swiped the pudding snack out of your lunch box.

It's up to your parents to keep your greed focused in more or less realistic directions. This is so that they can avoid the annoying expense of building roller coasters in the back yard.

Part I: Bikes, Docks & Slush Nuggets

As you enter your teens your material dreams escalate, but you also begin to realize on your own that the chances are pretty good that you won't be getting that army-surplus UH-1 helicopter or those skydiving lessons. You begin to adjust your desires accordingly. Not completely though, because you keep dreaming of dirt bikes and dune buggies until well into your twenties.

Once you have kids of your own, all bets are off. You are so busy stepping into your parents' role and managing your child's expectations that you no longer have time to nurture any of your own. And the cool thing is that you really don't need any – you find that whatever you are able to do to light up their eyes is way more fun than anything you could have wanted for yourself. I think this might be something that's hard-wired into the parenting genes.

So I guess the bottom line is, I already possess pretty much all the material things I need. I have all the basic dad tools, like a great grill, a snazzy lawn mower, and a cordless drill. I have some really extravagant luxuries like an iPod and a chrome-plated steel guitar. I even have a car with just a few payments left on it, a boat with no payments left on it, and my torn Barefoot Company t-shirt.

And I have a family who loves me. Life really doesn't get any better than that.

Coming Soon:

What I've Learned So Far...
Part II: Angels, Chimps & Tater Mitts

Made in the USA
Charleston, SC
19 November 2009